Laura Busini Birch was born and brought up in Mussolini's Italy in Fabriano, central Italy. She earned her degree in classics at the University of Rome. She met her husband, a major in the Royal Artillery, during the fighting in her home town, when the British Eighth Army, pushing its way through Italy, freed the country from the Fascist and German occupation. At the end of the war they married and she came to live in England in 1946.

Having taught herself English, she spent many years teaching in a primary school. She has two daughters, lives in London, but has a second home in Italy.

Laura Busini Birch

Traditional
Italian Food

This edition published 1996 by Diamond Books
77-85 Fulham Palace Road
Hammersmith
London W6 8JB

First published 1985 by Fontana Paperbacks

Printed in Great Britain

Acknowledgements

Any achievement, however small and humble, is the result of a collective effort. *'L'unione fa la forza'*, 'Union produces strength', says an Italian proverb. So my thanks and appreciation go to all the friends and members of my family, here and in Italy, who have encouraged and assisted me in this venture, particularly my husband, and my daughter Ann, who scrutinized my writing with sound judgement and critical eye, and my daughter Diana who translated the Italian poem on wine into English verse (page 44).

The author and publisher are grateful to Arti Grafiche Gentile for permission to reproduce drawings of Fabriano.

Contents

Introduction

If you are one of those fastidious persons whose culinary taste does not venture outside the twelve-mile limit around the British Isles, and shudder at the thought of not only eating, but cooking Italian food, do not read on; this book is not for you.

It is meant for people who already know what Italian food is about, appreciate it, and are prepared to try more unusual dishes, especially the traditional ones that Italians like to eat at special times of the year, at festivals and family celebrations. You need to be a very lucky tourist and be in the right place at the right time in Italy to succeed in trying them all.

Spend two or three weeks' holiday in an ordinary hotel anywhere in Italy and what will you get? Dishes that only vaguely resemble the people's food. Sometimes they try to please the foreigners by giving them what they think they like in their own country. For instance, you will get coffee which is not coffee at all (most of the time it is made with roasted barley or chickpeas), and since the arrival in Italy of the ubiquitous German tourists, in some cases the quality of food is sacrificed for quantity.

There are some very good Italian restaurants in London, but I am not one for trusting new places on recommendation or advertising. I shall never forget the day I was out with the family, and we felt like a good plate of spaghetti at lunchtime. There was a well-known Italian place nearby, so we went in. The dish was inedible by Italian standards, and when I protested to the Italian waiter, 'Just tell me, would you eat this stuff?' he replied, 'Oh no, I couldn't. We all go and eat in a small place in the next street!'

Across the world, I carefully avoid Italian restaurants: the further you are from Italy the worse they seem to be. We must not forget that those people are there to make enough money to go back home as quickly as they can, and the majority of Italian immigrants are usually very homesick. They will scrape and save until they are able to return with enough money to spend the rest of their life there. I knew an Italian lady who returned to her home town after having been away, working very hard, for twenty-five years. When she came back her comment was, 'The feeling I liked best was walking those streets again, but this time with money in my pockets!'

Italian dishes vary, of course, from region to region, but I will try to keep to the ones more common to the country as a whole. A dish like *cappelletti* (little hat-shaped pasta) served in capon broth makes me think straightaway of snow at Christmas time, together with roast turkey on the spit, *torrone* (nougat) and *panettone* (light fruit cake); while eel, mostly roasted, is a treat reserved for Christmas Eve, lasagne for family celebrations, ravioli for Easter, and on a cold winter's day you may crave for a warming plate of steaming polenta.

Italian meals, no matter how ordinary, will always be a three-course affair. In everyday life there will be no *antipasto*, but the meal will begin either with a *pastasciutta* or a soup, then there will be a 'main' course, followed by fruit. As with everything else, customs differ from north to south. Northerners will tend to cook a big lunch, then have a more frugal evening meal, while in central and south Italy dinner in the evening will be more substantial than the midday meal. *Colazione* means breakfast, but, as breakfast usually consists of just a cup of coffee or very little more, in more refined circles *colazione* indicates lunch, while *pranzo* is an evening meal. Ordinary folk will call *pranzo* the midday meal and *cena* the evening one. *Pranzo* is also a celebration feast. A bit confusing, don't you think? But useful to know, just in case you are invited to *colazione*. You would find it a bit embarrassing to turn up at eight o'clock in the morning!

When you sit down to an Italian meal, you will not hear any grace or prayer to thank anybody for our Daily Bread: the most you might hear is '*Buon appetito*' which, nowadays, is considered out of fashion, so the best thing to do is just to shut up and eat!

Apart from traditional recipes, I've included a range of dishes typical of my native land which I am sure will tempt Anglo-Saxon tastes also. They are all recipes which I have learned from my grandmother, my mother and my friends. They have had the approval and the praise of many very fussy Italian friends and very conservative British friends, so I hope I am providing good Italian recipes to suit everybody's taste.

I like to think of cooking as a pleasure not a chore. You may think that some of these dishes take long to make, but once you try them you will see that this is not so. Many can be prepared in advance, and most of them (marked with the symbol Ⓕ) freeze well, so you can make something special for your dinner parties with hardly any work on the day. I shall try to explain everything step by step in all my recipes, because there are always some points which are new territory, even for an experienced cook. Even men unaccustomed to cooking should be able to follow my instructions. My husband was my guinea pig, but only for the easiest recipes, because he is not a cook at all. I once went away for a few days and, as usual, left dinners in the freezer with every possible instruction for their use. When I came back he told me that one evening he wanted to cook some sausages from the freezer. His comment was, 'I grilled them but they would not cook in the middle.' 'Did you not turn them on the other side?' I asked. 'Oh yes,' he replied, 'but they still would not cook.' He proceeded to show me how he had cooked his sausages: one whole packet under the grill, six sausages in a bundle, the way you buy them. Can you be more of a beginner than that?

Italians are very hospitable and they will be generous in excess towards guests and friends. Even in hard times, like during the war, when it was everyone for himself, they would make every effort to welcome unexpected visitors. It is part of Italian nature to show off and give more than they can afford. Italians never make portions, but always bring food to the table and, as my mother taught me, there must be some left over to be sure that there was enough to start with.

A peculiarity of Italian politeness is that they will very rarely accept something you are offering for the first time. Italians will say 'No, thank you' to the first offer, and will only accept – if they want to – after the offer has been repeated. Before I got used to British ways, I would always say 'No, thank you' at first, and wait to be asked again – which of course I wasn't!

I would not want to be accused of encouraging people to eat unhealthy food, with too much fat, when we are always being reminded of the hidden dangers to our wellbeing in so many gorgeous dishes. You can always substitute the type of fat I use in my recipes with whatever you feel your heart desires: polyunsaturated fats can take the place of ordinary margarine or butter or lard, and the same goes for frying oil. Bear in mind that it is a medical fact that people living in the poorer parts of Italy, in the south, where the diet consists mostly of pasta, olive oil, bread, lots of vegetables, little meat and hardly any butter, have a lower incidence of heart attacks than the population from the more affluent northern part of the country. A doctor also told me that a little wine lowers your blood cholesterol. So, let your common sense prevail, keeping in mind that we cannot starve our bodies of everything, and enjoy eating your Italian dishes without the sense of guilt that accompanies forbidden foods.

By the end of the last war we had been so starved of fats for some years that we were craving for rich, fatty foods. One of my favourite snacks was a sandwich, made with a thick layer of margarine, which no one could mistake for butter, and slices of uncooked tinned bacon, both army issues, which the troops very gladly got rid of and which found their way to our tables through the flourishing black market of those days.

When the British troops were in my town, my family invited to dinner some officers who were billeted in the house next door and seemed to be very interested in Italian food. We managed somehow to produce a sumptuous meal, which surprised even us, because we did not know at first how we were possibly going to cope. The guests seemed to enjoy everything and thanked us profusely. Strangely enough, some of them were not very well the next day. We did not connect the event with the food when we heard this, because we had all eaten the same things and we were in perfect good health. In fact, better than usual, as we had not had a meal like that for a long time. Only a few years later, when I was living in London, my husband told me the secret of that strange malady. Thinking that 'the poor Italians' would give them a lousy meal, they all had a full officers' mess dinner, before coming to our house. Of course, then their eyes were bigger than their stomachs and they could not resist eating all the good food we had prepared. Hence the 'sick' feeling, a sort of unknown 'legionnaire's disease' with a difference!

My home town, Fabriano, is in central Italy, in the Marches region. I love talking about my birthplace, but I shall try to be careful that enthusiasm for my native land does not alter the truth. Fabriano is a well-known town, situated about 200km (150 miles) northeast of Rome. If you

Piazza Alta, Fabriano

draw a straight line from Rome to Ancona (a port on the Adriatic Sea), you will find Fabriano just over the Apennine mountain range. So the town has the Apennines to the west, and hills and other mountains of secondary ranges on the other sides, giving the impression that it is sitting in a bowl at 354m (1318 feet) above sea level. The countryside is of particular interest, with its mountains rising to 6000 feet, hills and gorges, its vegetation and remote mountain villages, typical of that part of Italy. Fabriano also, because of its position, is an ideal centre from which to go on and visit lots of other interesting places: Florence, Rome, Assisi, Perugia, Urbino and Ancona, for example.

The climate can be very pleasant in spring and autumn, with some extreme temperatures in winter and summer. There are a few weeks of snow every winter, and sometimes some very hot summers. Things have changed a lot from the time when people in villages could be cut off for months in the winter, but it can still be a very unpleasant experience to be caught in a snow blizzard on one of those mountain roads.

In small provincial towns like Fabriano, some of the things going on are very peculiar to visitors. For example, walking along the main street of the town (il Corso), just as it gets dark, is a usual thing for people young, and not so young, to do. There will be couples, rows of boys, girls and all sorts of people, going from one end of the street to the other end, turning round and coming back again. They will meet, shake hands (in Italy you shake hands when you meet and when you part, even if only a brief moment has passed between the two actions), stop and chat, then resume their antics walking up and down! This will go on until the time comes for them to go home to dinner.

This walk in the evening, '*il passeggio della sera*', is something of a parade: girls will wear their best new clothes; they will show off their new shoes, their hairdos – anything that might attract the attention of their male counterparts. This custom must be peculiar to Italy, as I have never noticed it anywhere else – except when I was in Zara (Yugoslavia) once, but then I realized this town had been part of Italy until the last war!

Fabriano grew from a Roman colonization. The first nucleus of people who installed themselves on the banks of the River Giano (from Janus, a Roman god with two faces) were some *fabbri* – smiths. According to legend, there were two groups of settlers, one on each side of the river. A bridge was between them and the smithy was nearby. The two groups were fighting, very often being a nuisance to the blacksmith who was in the middle, so he intervened with remarkable diplomacy until the two merged into one group. They showed their gratitude to 'Mastro Marino', the smith, by adopting his effigy in the shield of the new town. The name Fabriano, despite the coincidence of the Latin word *faber* (a smith), does not derive from the shield, but from a certain Faberius, an ancient Roman settler, who owned an estate in the countryside.

Fabriano's shield

Introduction

Since its birth, many industries have flourished along the banks of the river that flows through Fabriano. All through the centuries, this has helped to make it a prosperous place to live in. Some of its early industries have gone into decline and disappeared, like hat-making for the clergy, for example. Fabriano's artisans were proud hat-makers, not only for ordinary priests but also for cardinals and popes. Every new pope was presented with a hat from Fabriano as soon as he was elected.

Other industries have prospered in their place, but the one for which Fabriano is famous is the paper industry. Its paper mill is reputed to have been the first in Europe. Paper-making started before AD 1000 and has been a flourishing art throughout the centuries, apart from some brief times of economic depression. Fabriano's paper is renowned all over Italy and the world, especially the hand-made paper (*carta a mano*) which is still produced. '*Faber in amne cudit, olim cartam undique fudit*' is the motto on the town shield – 'The smith worked on the river and at one time paper from there was sent everywhere'. Watermarks for banknotes were also invented here.

Some people are still dedicated to agriculture, but only on a very small scale as the land is not very fertile. It is mostly grazing land; the winters are too severe for the commercial cultivation of things like fruit and vegetables, which grow plentifully just a few kilometres away towards the Adriatic Sea.

The population of Fabriano is now about 26,000, taking into account the surrounding villages, some of which are still remote and primitive. Only a couple of years ago, when I visited one of these little villages, I was talking to a housewife who was telling me about her house being modernized. She invited me in and proudly showed me the latest additions: a lavatory and a fridge. The latter had been given the place of honour in their best room (*la sala* – the parlour). I congratulated her and asked if I could see inside

Paper making by hand

Choosing the rags

Shredding the rags into fibre

Sizing hand-made paper with animal glue

the fridge. 'Of course!' she said, and opened it. I then saw that it was still brand new, but empty – not even connected. When I asked her why she was not using it she said, 'Well, we possess a fridge now, but we cannot yet think what to put in it!'

Another family I know in the same village lived for years in a house which was like a barn, terribly poor and dirty; a sort of stable, shared with chickens, cats, rabbits and hens. Their only ambition in life was to build a new home and this they accomplished after years of hard labour shared by all the members of the family, parents and children alike. Their new house is a showpiece: it stands next to their old house, like a villa, with a beautiful walled garden, gates, all clean and modern, but – because they had been used to living rough – it is now too good for them to live in! They are happy to admire their new home and to show it off proudly to visitors. But, as for moving in, that is another matter . . .

After friends and relatives tried to persuade the man of the house to occupy it, he made a resolution: when his eldest daughter got married he would make her wedding day the inauguration day for the house – a marvellous day when he would open the house to everyone in the village and they would have the best party ever, with no expense spared. But . . . they woke up one morning to find that their daughter had eloped with a fireman, so the beautiful house is still not yet in use!

People still use something called '*il prete*' (the priest) to warm up the bed on cold winter's nights. Much more efficient than a brass warming pan, it consists of a wooden frame which holds the bedclothes apart, and a ceramic bowl (*la monaca* – the nun) full of cinders and hot charcoal embers, which is placed in the middle. It takes about half an hour to warm up the bed as effectively as any electric blanket would.

Fabriano belonged to the Papal States from 1442 to 1860,

when it became part of the newly formed Kingdom of Italy under King Victor Emmanuel II. It still has all the characteristics of a medieval town, with the walls, four gates, turrets, *vicoli* (very narrow streets), the triangular *piazza alta* (high square) to distinguish it from the *piazza bassa* (lower square or market square). In the *piazza alta* are the palaces where the rulers, *I Signori*, lived (twelfth to thirteenth century) and the beautiful *fontana sturinalto* (high spouting fountain) dating back to 1088. The market square has lost its arches due to bombing during the Second World War and has changed a little, but the high square has been preserved as an historic centre. Churches are numerous there, and each one has its own interesting features.

Fabriano has been the cradle of some well-known painters, its most famous son being Gentile (fourteenth century). Unfortunately, none of his paintings is left in his native town: they are scattered all over the world, from Florence to Pisa, to Washington and the Queen's gallery in London.

Only since I've left have I appreciated the beauty and interest of my home town. Everything used to seem to me to be quite ordinary and I have been surprised when friends of mine (Fabriano is off the beaten tourist track) have expressed their admiration and delight at the sight, falling in love with the place immediately.

My ambitions used to be, first, to survive the war, then to see more of the world. My world until then had been confined to a very small part of Italy. I got hold of a book to teach myself English the day South African soldiers came to requisition part of our house. Next came the New Zealanders, and finally the British. By the time I encountered the Royal Artillery, I could speak a little, understand very little and my vocabulary was limited to words of everyday use and to useless phrases like 'down the hatch', 'mud in your eyes', 'Hello, beautiful' and so on! I

Fontana sturinalto

thought I was progressing well with my new language until one day an officer came to my house and spoke a lot. But he went away in despair: not one word had I understood. I was really frustrated, but then I solved the mystery. I saw him again, and he was part of a group of soldiers *in gonnella* ('mini-skirted'), who everybody went to see on parade each morning in the main square. That gave me encouragement. Obviously, I said to myself, they do not speak the same language as the other soldiers! I never expected then that I would get to know and to understand the Scots so well, until one of my daughters moved to Scotland.

I was asked to show the most interesting parts of my town to two officers, who were looking for a place to install their sergeants' mess. As we were walking along, I was trying my best with my limited English, while a very animated conversation was going on between the other two. I could not understand anything except the word 'camera', which kept coming up. Now, in Italian *camera* means bedroom, so my suspicious nature was aroused, and with a very polite but decisive gesture, I made them understand that they would have to finish their sightseeing on their own. Only a few days later the misunderstanding was cleared up: I saw them with this object in their hands which they introduced as 'the camera'. I was so relieved that I readily agreed to have my photograph taken with them!

When I came to England my ambition was to learn the language properly and in a surprisingly short time I knew it well enough to start teaching. A friend of ours commented, 'All the children in the village will learn to speak with an Italian accent!' I never had any ambition to write a book. I am no writer and my English still has some rough patches which I am trying to iron out as well as I can. But this project started from noting down recipes for my friends from time to time and finding that many had a great interest in accounts of life in an Italian country town and my life there.

I have many friends here, and in Italy where I go as often as I can. All anecdotes in this book are true, and some of my friends will probably recognize themselves, but I hope they will take the joke in good humour and still consider me 'one of them'. There are still things that I have not taken to in England, even after so many years: rice pudding, a cup of tea (I have never made myself one, although I will drink it to be polite), a game of cricket and commenting on any movement of the clouds – because in Italy we never talk about the weather! The first time a neighbour stopped me in the street just to say 'Isn't it lovely?' while pointing upwards to a small triangular patch of blue sky, I thought she must have escaped from the nearest asylum. I felt like a girl I knew who went to work in Ancona, a large town which had the only asylum in the area. She had gone out shopping when my aunt, whom she was working for, saw her running into the house in a state of shock and fear. 'There is a madman escaped from the "Red Roofs"' (the local name for the asylum). My aunt tried to calm her down, asking her some questions. Where did she see this man? Had he approached her? 'No, no, but he was gesticulating in the middle of the road, trying to get a lift from the cars!' The poor girl had never seen a policeman on traffic duty!

Although modern life with its travelling facilities has brought different countries so near to each other, obliterating many differences in the customs and ways of living, there are always things that will startle a foreign eye at some point or another. At births, weddings, funerals and other religious ceremonies, traditions will still emerge even when people have been influenced by modern times. 'What is the meaning of the enormous, beautiful bow, made of ribbons of tissue paper, hanging on somebody's front door?' A new baby has been born and the ribbons will be either pink for a girl or blue for a boy. 'What are those notices on the walls all over town?' Some are notices from the council to the public: the ones framed in heavy black lines are notices of death. They are put up within a couple of hours of somebody's death, which is perhaps a macabre custom, but you must remember that in Italy funerals usually take place the next day. At times of extreme temperatures (very hot or very cold) there is a veritable rash of such notices.

Religion plays a great part in Italy's life but people will observe some customs, not necessarily because they are so devout, but because the whole social structure of the country has been influenced by the Roman Catholic church for so many centuries. Very few are the number of people with extreme left political views who will dare to break the tradition of a church wedding. Very fervent communists will have their children baptized and you will find that they will expect their family to bury them after a religious service, although they will probably want to be laid in their coffin wearing a red tie. Nearing the day of reckoning their best policy is to keep on good terms with God and the Red Flag alike! It is considered sad and shameful to have somebody of your family buried 'in the field'. The field is part of the cemetery which belongs to the council, where people of no means are buried. Anybody else will make sure that their dear departed have a place in some built-up tomb, bought by the family, and the more you go up in the social scale, the better your family place in the cemetery. You start with individual 'ovens' (*fornetti*), small slots big enough for one coffin, built up into a wall, like a built-in oven, then you get the bigger sort of mausoleums, which belong to whole families.

My husband could not get over this, when I took him along to see the newest cemetery in my town. Some people have places that equal their homes or even better. They look like little studio bungalows, beautifully kept, polished and shiny. And often on a Sunday there is a pilgrimage of people who not only visit their family places, but the real fun for them is to walk about to see what the other tombs look like and which ones are kept better than others. It is a sort of 'keeping up with the Joneses' or oneupmanship being continued after death.

There will always be things you miss about your country of origin, no matter how long you have been away. On a summer's day I miss waking up to the garrulous singing of the swallows, darting ceaselessly, high in the sky – a sound that tells you it is a beautiful clear day. I miss the sound of the crickets, the cicadas in the countryside, the fields alight with fireflies, the aromatic perfume of my mountains, the Apennines in winter, topped with crisp snow and the blinding, bright sunlight of a winter's day. These are the things I will always miss.

Feste   *Festivals*

Many Italian dishes relate specifically to festivals and family occasions. Indeed, any excuse for Italians to mark a date with a celebration at the table is welcome.

CARNEVALE   *Carnival Time*

Carnevale is the time of the year between 17 January and Ash Wednesday, the beginning of Lent. In some areas it is celebrated more than in others; in Italy the Venice and Viareggio carnivals are famous, although this custom as a whole is being revived throughout the country. There are street parties, dances in fancy dress, some depicting the characters of the *maschere* from the *Commedia dell'arte* which date from the sixteenth century. In those days people were permitted to dress up as Pantalone, Arlecchino, Pulcinella and so on, and would speak in their dialect. Carnival is a time of enjoyment and good food, when many excesses are permitted before the lean time of Lent. *'Di carnevale ogni scherzo vale'* – 'at carnival time any joke is allowed' is the literal translation of this popular proverb.

The word *carnevale* comes from *carne levare* (to take meat away), because at midnight Lent begins with many meatless days. The days from the carnival period which are most celebrated are the last Thursday before Lent, *giovedì grasso* (fat Thursday), then the following Sunday, and finally the Tuesday which is called just 'Carnival Day' and corresponds to Shrove Tuesday.

For one whole year during the war, we had to take refuge in a mountain village, which we already knew very well and where everybody was very friendly. There were lots of

other families from the town and the very hospitable
country people had found room to accommodate a very
great number of extra 'refugees'. In the normal days
boredom was relieved only by the fascinating spectacle of
Flying Fortresses in formation, by the occasional bomb, or
by a couple of Mosquitoes (dive bombers, not insects,
although we would have preferred the latter), or by
somebody shouting '*Ecco i Tedeschi*' ('The Germans are
coming').

Carnival Day was going to be another one of those days,
without anything more exciting to brighten it up. We were
just passing the time talking, playing cards, telling jokes,
when suddenly I had an idea. There was a young fellow in
the village who had lived in the town for the last few years
and had only come back because of the war, but who did
not want to be considered one of the villagers. He thought
himself too good for that. Well, I thought, it is time to give
him a lesson.

I knew that some people would play cards during the
afternoon in one of the houses and that he would be over
the moon to be invited there. I made all the arrangements,
with the help of a couple of girls from the village who acted
as couriers. I called my brother, who was then about
thirteen years old – quite handsome, no beard yet – and told
him of my plan. He tried hard to get out of it, but when I
reminded him that when the schools opened again I would
be his schoolmistress, he had no choice but to do what I
was asking him. I was a last-year university student, but
the schools were so short of teachers with all the men
away, that the Education Authority had resolved the
problem by employing students.

I dressed up my brother as well as I could with my
clothes, and with clothes borrowed from other girls. His
short hair was the difficult part, but I managed to bring it
forward like a fringe and I put a scarf around his head in
a way which was fashionable for those days. A young man

accompanied my brother in disguise to the house where they were playing cards and where our victim had been invited. My brother, under the name of Clara, was introduced to the gentleman in question. He was immediately so taken by her charms that he invited her to go with him to his house where he summoned his mother to make a special plate of *castagnole* (page 252 for the recipe). His mother, too, was pleased for her son, while my poor brother was only thinking of how to get out. Very soon one of us went to Clara's rescue, saying she was expected for dinner, and brought her back home, but not before she had agreed to meet the same gentleman the next afternoon. Next day came and Felice (Happy was his very inappropriate name) was waiting impatiently for his date to show up. More and more people gathered around him, until somebody asked what he was waiting for. After general request, I transformed my brother right in front of Felice into the girl of his dreams, and then he realized that we had played a carnival joke on him. He just went away, disappeared without a word, and, like in the fairy tales, none of us ever saw him again.

PASQUA *Easter*

Easter is one of the few times of year when Italians have eggs for breakfast and a great quantity of eggs are used at this time of the year, mainly to make omelettes, with the fresh herbs that grow wild in the spring, and special types of cakes. In all Italian villages, towns and even in the cities, there is the custom of the 'blessing of the houses' during the Holy Week. Every parish priest has an area to visit, and the housewives are terribly busy spring-cleaning in preparation for the day the priest is due. With a certain pride the best bedspreads will be put in use and everything will be spick and span for Dom Romualdo, or whoever it will be. The priest is accompanied by a boy holding the tools of the trade (holy water and incense) and he will collect a basket of fresh eggs, cakes and any money that people give for the Easter celebrations. The money will go to the Church, while the other items will be shared between the priest and the boy.

You might think that performing this duty would mean a sort of apprenticeship to priesthood. Nothing of the kind! As a matter of fact, it seems that such a duty puts them off the whole idea once they grow up: there are many young men that I remember as children who used to be inseparable partners to priests on these occasions, and who are now very much involved in anything but religion!

The Easter breakfast table will have boiled eggs, and the new season *salame* will be started. The children's eggs will be painted, while the chocolate ones will be reserved for later in the day. Chocolate eggs always have a surprise inside them; the less expensive ones will have trivial things, rather like Christmas crackers in Britain (they do not have crackers at all in Italy), but the expensive ones can have valuable presents in them.

The *colomba* is the typical Easter cake, made in the shape of a dove. It is a very light cake with sultanas and candied peel, cooked with a sort of sugary crust and almonds. There are many recipes for homemade cakes, called *pizze* in many areas, either sweet, with currants or sultanas, or with cheese. In this case *pizza* means 'cake' and has nothing to do with the *pizza napoletana* that everybody knows.

ONOMASTICI

Onomastico is the day on which a saint's name is celebrated. If you look at an Italian calendar, you will find that every day has one saint, sometimes even two (of course the number of saints increases while the number of days stays still, and some of the days are getting a little crowded!). Different calendars do not always agree on a particular saint for the same day. Only the best-known ones are kept to the same date, like Saint Peter, John, Paul, Mary and so on. If you happen to have one of the best-known names of the martyrology (martyrology is the history and collection of names of martyrs and saints), then you have an extra day to celebrate – your *onomastico*. An affectionate Italian way of wishing a member of the family 'Happy Birthday' is to give a gentle pull to his or her ears while saying '*Auguri*'. But Italians make more of a fuss over well-known *onomastici* than over birthdays. Of course, often the *onomastico* and birthday coincide, because the person was named after the saint on whose day he was born. If you are unlucky and your parents have given you a name unknown to religious celebrations, then you better make the best of your birthday. Otherwise, you can always say that your name appears in *your* particular calendar! I have never found a saint with my name, so I cannot celebrate an *onomastico*, although I was christened with seven names.

It was sad when Saint Christopher was somehow demoted by Pope John XXIII from his position as patron saint of travellers, following some reorganization of the saints' hierarchy (perhaps the calendars were getting too crowded). On that day (25 July) there used to be a very unusual procession in Fabriano: the procession of all the cars in the town. They would meet in the main square, tour the streets bumper to bumper, sounding their horns incessantly (a real Italian-style affair, noisy to excess), and they would end up at the little church of Saint Christopher situated at the north gates of the town for the blessing of the vehicles. The parish priest would stand outside the church as the cars stopped, one by one, and the drivers received a Saint Christopher's medal to put on the car's dashboard, while in return each participant gave an offering for that church. In the evening there were Saint Christopher's dinners all over the town.

NOZZE *Weddings*

The first time I went to an English wedding I heard people talking about confetti, but I was surprised when I found that these confetti were paper petals which you throw on the happy couple. In Italy confetti are white sugared almonds which have come to be associated with weddings in the same way as orange blossom. 'When are we going to eat your confetti?' you may ask an engaged couple. In the small villages, after a wedding ceremony, the couple will walk back to the house where the wedding lunch will be held and as they come out of the church they will throw around handfuls of sugared almonds, to the excitement and delight of children and adults alike. Sugared almonds are expensive, so they will probably mix them with confetti *cannellini*, which are small white confetti made with sugar and a small piece of cinnamon in the middle instead of an almond.

When I was on holiday in Italy once, I was invited to a wedding which was quite unique. The bride was a girl who lived in a mountain village and had looked after my sister some years before, so she was like one of the family. But there was no bridegroom. A couple of months earlier the priest from a village on the other side of the mountain had come over with the news that some of his young parishioners had been engaged by a firm to go to work in Tierra del Fuego in Argentina. They had been there for a while and were feeling very lonely in that desolate place, so they had asked the priest to find them some girls of good character willing to marry them and go and live over there.

The excitement which this request aroused was indescribable. Going abroad for some people is like winning first prize in a lottery (no thought was given to the fact that people have to work just as hard 'abroad' to get by, or to what sort of place Tierra del Fuego would be for these poor girls). My first reaction was to tell Amalia to open her eyes, but she seemed so sure that she'd be happy that I kept quiet.

And so the ceremony took place, with the bridegroom's brother acting as the groom. People gave very generous presents, taking into account that they would probably never see Amalia again. Soon the trunks were ready and all that was left was to wait for a passage on the boat to Argentina. This came a couple of months later, but Amalia was not feeling very well (she was probably getting cold feet) and decided to wait for the next boat.

We had underestimated her. She was intelligent enough to wait for news from the unfortunate girls who went ahead of her to meet their husbands. When the next boat was ready to sail, Amalia was not, and she announced that she would stay where she was. This nearly caused a war between the two villages, but Amalia's good sense prevailed, and with the help and advice of friends, she managed to get the marriage annulled. And the presents? They came in very handy when she married again and set up home with a childhood sweetheart!

Any wedding feast, be it breakfast or lunch, is a very long affair. A typical wedding lunch menu might be:

Antipasto – mixed preserved meats in winter or *prosciutto*, melon and figs when in season, then a mixture of different pasta dishes to suit everybody: tortellini or cappelletti in broth, *lasagne verdi*, *tagliatelle alla panna*.

This will be followed by a platter of mixed fried meat: *cotolette* of veal, baby lamb cutlets, mixed fried vegetables and some green beans or spinach. If it is easy to get fish, there will probably be a dish of fried *calamaretti*.

A variety of roast meats will follow: roast beef, pigeon, lamb, for example, served with a green salad, or green tomato salad.

The sweet will be the wedding cake, which is usually a Saint Honorè, never a fruit cake. It will be in two tiers and will be cut by the bride just as it is done in Britain. As a matter of fact, the tradition of cutting the cake was imported after the last war. Fruit and coffee will follow.

There are no speeches, just toasts. At the end of the lunch, confetti will be distributed, and the bride and groom will go around to each one of the guests distributing one spoon of sugared almonds. The groom holds the bowl, and the bride has a silver spoon. They usually give five confetti each, which is considered as bringing good luck. Often confetti are wrapped in small squares of white tulle, tied with a white ribbon. Together with the five confetti there will be a small card with the names of the couple and an orange blossom, or some other flower. In this case, each guest will receive one bag. The friends that have not been able to attend but have bought a present will be sent a tulle bag of confetti placed in a small container of pottery, china or even silver, called *bomboniera*.

The expense of a wedding is shared equally by the two families, so there is no question of feeling lucky if you have just sons and no daughters. The tradition is that the bridegroom must also pay for the bride's dress. It is supposed to be unlucky if he doesn't, but that is certainly a good way of making a reluctant groom fork out the money!

SAN MARTINO *Saint Martin's Day*

Saint Martin's Day, 11 November, is another day remembered by gourmets in Italy. By tradition it is the day when the new wine is tasted: '*Per San Martino ogni mosto diventa vino*' – 'By Saint Martin's Day all the must will be wine' is the popular saying. It is usually drunk to wash down roast chestnuts. Do not forget when you cook chestnuts to make an incision on the skin so that they do not burst during cooking. It is not essential to have an open fire to be able to cook them. They are just as good baked in a hot oven or boiled until tender.

Saint Martin's Day is also called '*Festa dei cornuti*' (Cuckolds' Day). As the legend goes, it was the custom to make fun of men who were not lucky enough to have faithful wives and did nothing to safeguard their honour. Truths would come to light and betting would go on to decide who would gain the title of '*cornuto* of the year'. '*Cornuto*' literally means 'with horns'. During the day people light an enormous fire in the main square, to heat a great cauldron containing some mulled wine. Anybody passing by could have a hot drink to help them face the cold and fog which Saint Martin's Day is noted for. Nowadays mulled wine is not made in the middle of the square, although there is talk of reviving this custom.

VINO BRULÉ   *Mulled Wine*

1 litre (1¾ pints) red or white wine	6 cloves
½ teaspoon ground cinnamon	1 tablespoon sugar or honey
a piece of lemon and orange rind	

Place all the ingredients in a saucepan and bring slowly to the boil. Simmer for 10 minutes, add more sugar if desired, then strain and drink it hot.

EPIFANIA, ANNO NUOVO   *Epiphany, New Year*

Until some years after the war, the use of Christmas trees was almost unknown to the Italian people. The popular thing was to make a *presepio*, which is a scene of the birth of Jesus in a manger, with figures made in the local pottery and sold on a special market day, usually 13 December –

Saint Lucia's Day. The first ever *presepio* is attributed to Saint Francis of Assisi.

The custom of the Christmas tree in homes and in the main square of a town is very popular now, but no houses, offices or schools will have decorations as they do in the UK. One of the nicest customs of the festive season was to give presents – usually *panettone* and *spumante* – to policemen on duty on Christmas and New Year's Eve, propping them up against the box where they were standing. In these violent days you would probably be shot on sight if you tried to place a parcel at a policeman's feet!

Another custom that shopkeepers keep is to give a *strenna* (festive season present) to their regular customers. Unfortunately, this custom seems to be unknown to Italian shopkeepers here; they have readily adopted the more profitable custom of putting out a box for the customers to give!

Sending Christmas cards is not very common and you certainly would not send one to somebody living in the same town. Giving presents is mainly confined to children, not on Christmas Day, but on 6 January – Epiphany Day. Epiphany festival is the children's day, the day of the coming of the *Befana*, the old lady who brings presents during the night. She carries them in two huge baskets on her donkey. She is a very dear figure, dressed like an old-fashioned peasant woman with a long skirt, and a warm, woollen shawl that covers her from head to knees. She climbs down the chimneys to leave presents for children in their socks or pillow cases, or baskets. She will also invariably leave some homemade biscuits (pages 276). The *Befana* may have some of the supper left out for her and will take a carrot or an apple for her donkey.

Of course, at one time politics had to interfere even with this custom and in Mussolini's time there was the introduction of the *Befana fascista*, the state *Befana*, who would distribute presents to needy children in the afternoon, in the guise of one of the local dignitaries, accompanied by his wife, both dressed up in black *orbace*. This type of cloth, woven by Sardinian peasants, is thick and rather rough, and the Fascist Party adopted it as material for their uniforms, to revive the dying industry. The word *orbace* came to mean Fascist uniform.

On New Year's Eve, the night of San Silvestro, people will celebrate with an enormous midnight meal, a '*cenone di San Silvestro*'. The word *cenone* means 'big dinner'. A typical menu for a *cenone di fine d'anno* (big dinner at the end of the year) might be:

Antipasto of various *carni salate* (page 51)
Risotto con funghi (page 100)
Lenticchie con cotechino o zampone (page 214)
Panettone, torrone
Seasonal fruit
Caffé

At the stroke of midnight the *spumante* or Champagne corks will pop and everybody will wish each other '*Buon anno*'. In Italy people do not kiss; no man would kiss somebody else's wife, unless they are related. I have got used to the custom here where everybody seems to kiss everybody else, but if we have Italian guests, I have to drum into my husband's ear, 'Don't forget, you do not kiss Italian ladies.' Of course, he did forget on one occasion and I had to rush to his rescue explaining the different custom.

If you want to be lucky in the New Year, you should wear red panties and you should eat grapes at midnight. In the days when you could not get fresh grapes all the year round, we used to hang bunches on long poles and leave them in a dry place, usually in the loft, where they would keep until the festive season. If you eat grapes you are bound to count money, a lot of money during the next year. Unfortunately, to this date I have not found out whether you count money by spending it, by gaining it or by paying taxes! The latter would not worry Italians: they seem to be very successful in finding the best way to avoid paying them!

Are Italians superstitious? Yes, but in different ways from the British. You should never get married or start a new job on a Friday, but number 13 is not considered unlucky – in fact you can buy lucky charms with that number – and 17 is the number to avoid. A black cat does not bring you luck, especially if it crosses the road in front of your car, and to encourage good things to happen, you do not touch wood but iron, or you get hold of one of those red horns, made of coral or plastic! Horns made of precious metals or coral have always been sold as good luck charms and even the introduction of plastic has not diminished their power! And while the Anglo-Saxons cross their fingers to keep unfavourable happenings at bay, Italians make the sign of 'the horns', stretching out the index and little finger.

If a baby is born before the amniotic sac has broken, or '*con la camicia*' (literally, 'with his shirt on'), good fortune will follow him throughout his life.

Mercati *Markets*

In every Italian town square there is a daily fruit and vegetable market, while fish will be on sale probably two or three times a week if the town is away from the sea. To buy food at the market you have to get up early, because by eight o'clock the best has already gone. Peasants from villages near and far will not miss coming to town on market day. They used to either walk from miles away, or come in donkey and horse carts, but motorcycles and cars are now the more usual transport. But the market atmosphere remains unchanged.

There is a corner for everything. On one side you can buy live chickens, geese, ducks, rabbits, pigeons and eggs, then there is the corner for vegetables, pot plants, trees and flowers. Colourful stalls of the local produce will alternate with lorries which have brought the same things grown further away in the countryside. The prices are lower than in the shops, and you can pick and choose anything you want to buy: for example, you pick up the chickens to feel their breasts, and you must do the same for pigeons and rabbits (or you will be cheated), and you smell the melons. But you bargain in very few cases.

The weekly market, the day of which varies from town to town, is a colourful and larger affair when a greater number of tradesmen bring their wares. The merchandise offered appeals not only to the housewife, but to all the family. There will be linen, crockery, leather goods, clothes, shoes, garden and farm implements, tools of every type, toys, games, sweets. Ice creams will be sold in great quantities and there will be a greater variety of fruit and vegetables because the goods will also come from further away than on a normal day. One special sweet always sold at a market is *mandorlato*, a crunchy sweet with almonds and other nuts.

MANDORLATO   *Crunchy Almond Sweets*

225g (8 oz) almonds   *100g (4 oz) sugar*
100g (4 oz) hazelnuts   *100g (4 oz) clear honey*

Put the almonds in a saucepan, cover with water and bring to the boil. Remove the pan from the heat and take out the almonds, one by one, and peel off their skin. Place them on a baking sheet in an oven, preheated to 160°C (325°F), gas mark 3, and roast until a golden colour. Leave them to cool then cut them up in pieces. Place the hazelnuts on a baking sheet in the oven and lightly toast, then cool and chop them up. Mix the nuts together.

Place the sugar and honey in a saucepan over a high heat and boil until the mixture changes colour to caramel. Drop in the nuts and mix well until blended. Wet a baking sheet or a section of your worktop and pour the mixture on it, spreading it to a thickness of 1cm (½ inch). With a knife, mark some lines where you will cut when the mixture is cool. Leave it to get really cold before breaking into pieces along the lines.

Erbe aromatiche   *Herbs*

I never use herbs mixed in a bag (bouquet garni) in casseroles and stews. I like to see what kind, and how much, of each herb I put in: also I think herbs should be left in, not taken out like you would for a clove of garlic. By the time everything is cooked you can hardly find the small leaves and they add to the flavour. If you put a bag in, you will get the aroma, but there is always the danger you will forget to remove it from the dish.

ALLORO   *Bay Leaves (Laurus Nobilis)*

Not to be confused with the ordinary garden laurel. The very aromatic leaves are used a lot in cooking, and best used when fresh. Laurel has always been a symbol of glory, and a crown made with its leaves has been worn by poets, leaders and conquerors since early times. The origin of the laurel crown seems to be from Greek mythology. The very handsome Apollo fell in love one day with a pretty nymph, Daphne. She did not like his attentions and fled, but not quickly enough; Apollo was able to cast his spell changing her into a laurel bush, then he proceeded to cut one of the branches and made a crown for his head. In this way he could show off his conquest. Not a very heroic or glorious effort on Apollo's side, but in those days perhaps the passion and supernatural power of a god was equal to any mortal act of valour. And so the custom of crowning with laurel descended from the heights of Olympus to the lower parts of the then-known universe. The use of laurel leaves has spread to kitchens, boudoirs and bath water, making the laurel one of the most appreciated plants for its aromatic qualities.

BASILICO *Basil (Ocimum Basilicum)*
Basil will be found in every tin of Italian tomatoes as it is unthinkable to serve tomato sauce without the flavour of basil.

CAPPERI *Capers*
Capers are very common in Italy and grow in cracks in old walls facing south. You can buy them preserved in jars.

FINOCCHIO *Fennel (Foenicolum Dulce* and *Foenicolum Vulgare)*
There are two types of fennel: the cultivated one grows into a bulbous shape and is used in salads. The other grows wild, but you can grow it in your garden. The leaves, seeds and flowers are used with fish and meat.

AGLIO *Garlic (Allium Sativum)*
You will notice that my recipes require little use of garlic. Garlic must be used very carefully indeed. To rub the salad bowl or a roasting tin with a crushed clove is enough to give the flavour. Some people like to add to their salad a few chopped leaves from the growing garlic plant, which have a very mild flavour compared with the cloves. It is not true that all dishes from the continent, Italian in particular,

need garlic; in fact they are a minority, and, in nearly all my recipes, it should be removed at some point during cooking. I would like to add that, apart from keeping Dracula and your friends away, it is also supposed to keep high blood pressure at bay, hence its common description of 'poor people's doctor'.

During October, in nearly every town, there is a special market day – '*la fiera delle cipolle e aglio*' (the onion and garlic market) – when the produce of the recent harvest is sold. Onions and garlic are sold in great quantities, the dried stems being plaited into enormous lengths. These dry stems find their use, too; old men in the villages smoke them in their pipes to calm toothache! No wonder it is also called 'the farmer's chemist'.

MENTA   *Mint*
In Italy when mint is used, it is mostly the wild type.

PREZZEMOLO   *Parsley*
Parsley is much used in everyday Italian cooking. It can even help against insect stings, chopped up to cover the spot.

ROSMARINO   *Rosemary (Rosmarinus Officinalis)*
One of the most-used herbs is rosemary, and there is proof that it was appreciated since AD 300. The ladies of those days used it to preserve their youthful looks. Nowadays, it is an ingredient in many cosmetic preparations because of its perfume and tonic-like action. A bath with soaked rosemary leaves, yellow broom flowers and walnut leaves left overnight is supposed to give vigour and elasticity to your limbs.

SALVIA   *Sage (Salvia Officinalis)*
Sage is another indispensable herb in the kitchen. There is a saying, 'Why should he die if he has sage in his garden?'

It is supposed to be a digestive, tonic and stimulant, as well as being useful to whiten your teeth by rubbing a leaf on them. In ancient Egypt women used to drink boiled sage as a fertility drug.

ZAFFERANO *Saffron (Crocus Salivus)*
Originally from the East, saffron is grown commercially in the Piemonte region, but it will grow anywhere in Italy. In cooking it is used as a colorant, and you need 70,000 flowers to make 1kg of it!

Maggiorana (marjoram), *origano* (oregano), *santoreggia* (wild oregano), *timo* (thyme), *ginepro* (juniper). These herbs also find their way into Italian dishes, especially the wild types whose unforgettable aroma pervades the hills and the mountains. I try to have my little corner of Italian flavour in my garden, but I am afraid that most years it gets washed away with the rain.

Tartufi *Truffles*

Truffles have a characteristic, persistent odour, and a smooth skin with some protuberances, rather like potatoes. They are black outside with marble-like veins inside. Their size can vary from a walnut to an orange, and they reproduce by spores, like mushrooms. They grow wild, underground about 15–20cm (3–4 inches) down, and near to the roots of some particular trees, like oak, beech and hornbeam. During the last twenty years, the *Corpo Forestale* (Forestry Commission) has cultivated them artificially in specially prepared ground. It takes fifteen years before the truffles are ready to be gathered and they can be dug up with the help of trained dogs. Keen truffle hunters can apply for a licence to allow them to search for truffles.

The best type of black truffle grows on the central Apennines, around my home town. It has been called 'the diamond of the kitchen', mostly because of its price. You can use truffles to give special flavour to pasta, risotto, meat dishes and eggs. You scrape, wash and cut them in very thin slices, or just grate a little on top of your portion. One small truffle will go a very long way.

Agrumi   *Citrus Fruits*

Citrus fruits are cultivated extensively in the south of Italy a few miles south of Rome. Mandarin, lemon and orange groves are a wonderful sight when the trees are laden with fruit, but in the blossom season the pleasure they give is not only to the eyes; the perfume they exude is something out of this world.

Around Sorrento they are grown in terraces which date back to the Romans. At some time in the growing season the fruits need protection from the strong sun, and this is provided by pulling a light canopy over the trees.

Orange blossom always used to be a symbol for weddings and they provided an ornament for the brides, in the same way as for young vestal virgins in ancient Rome. Now I understand that the custom of orange blossom has changed to any flower the bride might fancy, disregarding the now inappropriate comparison with the vestal virgins.

The juice from fresh lemons is always handy to fight minor stomach ailments which often go with the heat of Italian summers.

Viti   *Vines*

Italy offers a variety of good and well-known wines for every occasion. Children start drinking a little wine when they are very small, usually with a little water. Although people drink at every meal, there is hardly any drunkenness; I had never seen anybody really drunk until the foreign troops appeared during wartime. The vine is cultivated all over Italy. It is said that Noah planted the first one and was the first person to discover the pleasant uplifting effect of its fermented juice, which since then has brought cheer and good humour to people's tables. I have even seen chickens having a day of euphoria when by chance they ate the remains of the lees after the wine making; they were lucky not to be killed on the spot because the farmer thought they had been affected by an unknown and very infectious disease! It is said that to get an abundant crop from your vines, it is good practice to bury the remains of dead animals nearby. A cheerful poet of the last century, Olindo Guerrini, left a spiritual testament saying:

> Quando morro'lungo la terra mossa,
> non piantate il cipresso e la mortella,
> io la mia tomba non la voglio bella,
> ma giovevole altrui piu' che si possa. . . .

> Piantateci una vite. Il suo giocondo,
> il suo celeste grappolo spremuto,
> diverra' vino ghiotto e rubicondo.
> E cosi' benche' morto, il mio tributo
> ai vivi paghero', rendendo al mondo
> qualche goccia del vin che gli ho bevuto.

When earth's disturbed upon my death
Plant not myrtle on my grave

Nor cypress beauty will I have
But joyful use of mother earth.

Plant there a vine
Whose heavenly fruit, when squeezed
Yields ruby drops of wine.
Thus my tribute to the living
I, though dead can still repay
To the world my wine I'm giving.

Formaggi *Cheeses*

There are many types of Italian cheese for eating and cooking, but I will limit my list to some of the best known.

PARMESAN cheese (*Parmigiano*) is made with cow's milk and is one of the best-known Italian cheeses abroad. It originated in Parma, hence its name, and the best types are *reggiano* and *lodigiano*.

PECORINO cheese (from *pecora* – sheep) is made with ewe's milk, and is supposed to have a special flavour because it is made with the milk from the sheep that have grazed on the Apennine mountains, which are rich in aromatic herbs. You can get all sorts of different *pecorino*, from every region, each with its individual taste or peculiarity of the area. PECORINO ROMANO comes from the plains around Rome and has the strongest flavour of its kind. PECORINO SARDO (from Sardinia) is mild. There is also the PECORINO SICILIANO (from Sicily) which has whole peppercorns in it. A mixture of cow and sheep's milk makes a soft cheese to eat fresh, called CACIOTTA. *Pecorino* cheese will be hard enough to grate about 8–10 months after making, and it must be kept in a dry room, on wooden slabs, and turned around each day. On polenta and some pasta dishes it is the rule to have grated *pecorino* instead of *Parmigiano*. Some people prefer *pecorino* all the time, like the people living in villages, who make their own. They will very seldom buy Parmesan, except for lasagne, because you cannot make a good dish of lasagne without Parmesan.

MOZZARELLA is fresh cheese made with buffalo milk. There are quite a few buffalo herds in the plains south of Rome and around Naples.

DOLCELATTE (sweet milk) is similar to Gorgonzola.

GORGONZOLA blue cheese, takes the name from the place Gorgonzola, near Milan.

PROVOLONE and CACIOCAVALLO are strong cheeses, made in the shape of a pear, from the Campania region.

MASCARPONE from Lodi (Milan) is a mild cheese, and is often used to make sweets.

GROVIERA, an imitation of the Swiss Gruyère.

STRACCHINO is a fresh and very soft cheese from Lombardia.

BEL PAESE ('beautiful country'), a mild, soft, creamy cheese.

Ricotta

Ricotta is not a cheese, contrary to what some people think, because it contains no casein. The milk and whey left over from making cheese still has enough substance to coagulate into ricotta. The ricotta you can buy is all right to use for cooking, but for eating as a dessert in its natural state, it is often too dry and heavy.

Ricotta can be eaten on its own, sprinkled with sugar, with sugar and a little liqueur, or mixed with fresh fruit cut in small pieces. If you find it difficult to obtain for cooking, the best thing to use is plain cottage cheese, without any flavour added, or some very mild cream cheese. If you live in the country you could perhaps obtain some ewe's milk and make your own ricotta.

You will need about 7–8 litres of ewe's milk to make a reasonable amount – a ricotta a little smaller than the ones you see in the shops – and you need to make cheese first. Warm the milk in a large saucepan and when it is just tepid, stir in 1 teaspoon of rennet (the substance that you buy from the chemist which will make the milk coagulate). Take the saucepan away from the heat, cover it and leave it until the milk coagulates. It will probably take more than an hour. With your hands, collect all the lumps, squashing them together to make a round of cheese about 15cm (7 inches) in diameter. Squeeze out as much liquid as you can, then strain all the liquid into another saucepan, to collect all the small pieces of cheese left, which you will add to the cheese round. Put the saucepan with the strained liquid on a very low heat. This liquid is slowly warmed up and brought to boiling point, but it must not go on boiling. It will have a thick layer of froth and curds on top. It is then strained through a very fine sieve or colander and left to drip until there is hardly any whey left. It is then turned out on to a plate and it will have the shape of the colander.

Frittate *Omelettes*

You can make omelettes using many different ingredients for the fillings. In fact, you can use almost anything: mint, asparagus, parsley, artichokes, chicory, courgettes, dandelions, sausages, mushrooms, fresh garlic leaves, spinach, beet, onions, aubergines, basil leaves, marrow flowers – no limit to what you can use to mix with the eggs to make a very tasty dish. I am only giving ideas of the things that make good *frittate*, which in the spring can have the addition of many wild herbs. I think even my husband should be able to clean and chop the vegetables, cook them for a few minutes in a little oil, and add the beaten eggs. Maybe, in fact certainly, he wouldn't be able to turn the omelette, but you can also eat it without turning; the result will be more moist and some people prefer it that way!

FRITTATA CON CIPOLLE E POMODORI
Omelette with Onions and Tomatoes

This is one of the omelettes I like best. It reminds me of a special time when I was expecting my first child and my husband would not call the doctor because he was insisting I had stomach trouble caused by eating one of these omelettes!

Serves 2

*1 large onion or 2 medium-
  sized
1 tablespoon margarine
salt and freshly ground
  black pepper*

*4 very ripe tomatoes
a few drops olive oil
3 eggs*

Peel and thinly slice the onions. In a non-stick frying pan, cook them in margarine until tender. Add salt and pepper. Dip the tomatoes in boiling water for a few moments, then skin, seed and finely chop them. Add them to the onions, season with more salt if necessary and stir, cooking for 15 minutes. Beat eggs well, with salt and pepper, and add to the mixture, adding a few drops of olive oil. Stir with a spatula and spread over the base of the pan, then turn the omelette and cook on the other side.

UOVA AFFOGATE   *Drowned Eggs*

Serves 4

225g (8 oz) tin peeled
   tomatoes
100ml (3½ fl oz) water
salt and freshly ground
   black pepper

1 teaspoon margarine
8 eggs

Strain the tomatoes through a sieve, so you have just the pulp and juice. Pour this juice into a frying pan with the water, salt, pepper and margarine and simmer for about 15 minutes. Bring rapidly to the boil, then add the eggs in, one at a time. (I would crack the eggs in a basin first. You never know, you may find a bad one which would spoil everything.) Keep boiling fast until the eggs are cooked.

FRITTATA AI FUNGHI   *Mushroom Omelette*

Serves 4

100g (4 oz) mushrooms
salt and freshly ground
   black pepper

corn oil
6 eggs

Prepare the mushrooms by wiping them clean with a damp cloth (do not soak them, because they get full of water). Slice them thinly. Season with salt and pepper, and fry with very little corn oil for about 10 minutes, stirring often. Beat the eggs with more salt, increase the heat under the frying pan and pour in the eggs. Stir gently. Turn the omelette when cooked on the underside. Place a large flat plate on top of the pan and invert the omelette on to it. Return to the pan and cook on the other side for a couple of minutes until set. Serve at once.

Pane   *Bread*

Making bread used to be a weekly task for any Italian housewife in the rural areas where you could not buy fresh bread. They would all make their loaves at the same time, line them up on a long board, cover them with a clean white cloth and a blanket (the bread must not be allowed to get cold), and take them along to a communal oven, balancing the boards on their heads. It used to be quite normal to see people carrying things this way, especially water pitchers. It is not too difficult once you have mastered it, providing you don't get a sudden urge to look at your feet.

Bread accompanies everything you eat in an Italian household and children are always told off for not eating enough bread. There will also be some *grissini* (breadsticks) on the table, because diet-conscious people think this will reduce their calorie intake, but they invariably end up eating both the bread and *grissini*. Very little brown bread is consumed and you can only buy it in a few places outside big cities. It is also difficult to find *pane a cassetta*, which is similar to loaves used for toast and sandwiches. *Pane all'olio* is considered to be the best bread.

1
Antipasti
Appetizers

Antipasto is a word which means 'before the meal' and not 'before the pasta', as some people may erroneously think, and it covers a whole range of appetizers.

Most *antipasti* consist of a variety of preserved meats which are called *carni salate*. Here is a list of common types of *carni salate* which you can use as appetizers.

PROSCIUTTO	Uncooked, preserved hind of pork, smoked in some regions. The best-known *prosciutto* is 'Parma ham'. (To make your own Parma ham, see page 53.)

SALAME	Mixture of lean pork meat and lard, finely minced together and preserved with salt, pepper and spices in skin (gut).
SALAME DI FABRIANO	This type of *salame* is typical of the town that gives its name. It is made from very finely minced lean pork, from the best cuts of meat, then mixed with a small quantity of lard, cut into very small cubes. It is seasoned with salt and whole peppercorns, then pushed into bags of gut. This is a very good type of *salame* and it is more expensive than others.
LONZA	Loin of pork, preserved in a similar way to *prosciutto*.
CAPOCOLLO	Literally 'top of the neck', shoulder preserved more or less in the same way. These last two types have a very similar taste to *prosciutto*, but they are less expensive.
MORTADELLA	Like a large *salame*, but it is the cheapest type, made with spiced minced pork, pieces of lard and peppercorns. It is said that *mortadella* was originally made with donkey meat.
COPPA (SOPPRESSA in some regions)	Cooked spiced pig's head, cut into small pieces, preserved in gut.
COTECHINO	These next two preserved meats are not used for *antipasti* as they need cooking, but are used in main dishes. *Cotechino* looks like a small *salame*, but it is very different, in the fact that the main ingredient in its making is the *cotica* or *cotenna* (skin) of the pig. The skin is put through a mincer a couple of times, then mixed with some lard and the cheapest cuts from the pig, and all

minced together. It is preserved with salt, pepper and spices in gut. *Cotechino* has to be boiled and is eaten hot. The most popular way of eating it is either with lentils (page 214), beans or polenta (page 169).

ZAMPONE *Zampone* is very similar to *cotechino*, but the meat mixture is stuffed into a pig's leg. (*Zampa* is the leg of an animal, *zampone* means a big one.) The best known is *zampone di Modena*.

There are lots of different types of *salame*: some have garlic; some a lot of garlic; others are spiced with a particular flavour; some are finely minced and some are of a very rough texture. The names vary with the regions. *Salame milanese* is the best for a non-Italian palate, but if you are adventurous and like to try regional specialities, the shopkeeper will very gladly advise you in line with your likes and dislikes. All Italian foodshops sell a variety of these meats. I have at times made my own, which is not a difficult thing to do, but you do need a place to hang them, which has to be at the right temperature with proper ventilation, and this is not usually possible in modern kitchens.

The best parts of the pig's gut are used to make salami and sausages. The end bits are cut off and cured in a special way with aromatic herbs (mainly fennel) and spices. They are delicious grilled. In my home town's dialect they are called 'ciarimboli', which literally means 'little bits'.

How to Cure Parma Ham

Have you ever wished you could make your own *prosciutto*, the type similar to the ham from Parma that is so expensive to buy? It is not at all difficult, providing you have a little patience and an unheated garage or cellar, or just a cold dry room, where you can hang it during its curing time.

The best time to start it is in September–October and it will be ready by the next summer. I remember when I was a child my parents used to get a very big, freshly killed pig from a farm, which was then brought into the house in two halves, placed on a table and left for about two days, head down, until all the blood was drained from the flesh.

After the blood had drained from the pig, the expert on the subject, called *il norcino*, would come to transform the gruesome carcass into mouthwatering fare. I used to be fascinated watching him work and I can still remember it all vividly. Now that you can buy whole or half pigs from many farms in the country, you can make many of those delicious things that are usually sold in delicatessens and Italian shops at home, at a fraction of the cost.

You do not have to buy a whole pig or even half of one to make your *prosciutto*. You only have to ask the farmer or the butcher to provide you with the whole of a hind leg of a pig, the bigger the better. The shape should be rounded at the top, showing just a bit of the bone of the hip joint. Cut off the trotter and make a hole where you can hang it from. Wash and carefully dry the leg. Rest it on a tray. Have ready a basinful of table salt and one of sea salt. Sprinkle the meat abundantly, first with the table salt, making sure you reach every bit of the leg, including the bone that shows, on all sides. A lot of the salt will fall off, but leave it on the tray, then sprinkle some sea salt over and under the ham, as well as on the skin, taking special care that the salt is sticking on to the bones and in every crevice. Leave the ham for forty days, turning it over every four or five days and adding a little more salt where it has melted.

After the forty days, lift up your ham, get a clean cloth,

dip it in wine and use it to wipe the salt off the ham. Mop up any moisture from it. Clean and dry the tray with a clean cloth, then dust the ham with ground black pepper. How much? Just make it black! Especially on and near the bones. Leave the ham flat on the tray for 3–4 days. Insert a big, strong 'S'-shape hook in the hole you made near the top end of the leg and hang it from the ceiling of your garage, or a dry, cool (not freezing) room. Make sure it does not touch anything. Check it every week or so at first, less later, and add more pepper if necessary. If there is any moisture forming wipe it with a vinegar-soaked cloth, dry it and add more pepper, lots of ground black pepper.

After about a month you can cover the ham with very fine muslin, but make sure some air gets to it. After a minimum of six months the ham should be ready, depending on its size and weight. You can check by cutting a small slice. The flesh should be dry. If it is moist and it has not yet acquired the dark pink-red colour of *prosciutto*, put more pepper on the cut and leave it for, say, another month. If you are in doubt, wait. It is better to wait a little longer than to cut it too early.

What satisfaction I felt the first time I started my own homemade ham here in London. I proved to my husband that it could be done in difficult conditions and limited space, after he had threatened to throw it away every time he walked in the garage and banged his head on it.

While you are consuming your ham, keep it covered with a cloth, especially the exposed part, and hang it again. Do not put it in the fridge or freezer. Always use a very sharp knife and cut it very thin. When you hit the bone, start cutting on the other side. If at any time, perhaps towards the end of it, the meat gets too hard and difficult to slice thinly, wrap it up with a damp cloth (a clean cloth, wrung out), and leave it for a day or so, renewing the operation if necessary. The flesh will soften and will cut very easily.

Antipasto al prosciutto
Hors d'Oeuvre with Parma Ham

Prosciutto is the *antipasto par excellence*. It is the Italian answer to Scottish smoked salmon. You can serve it on its own with crusty bread, or with melon (preferably pink flesh but any melon will do), or, best, with fresh green or dark figs. You can roll the sliced ham into sausage shapes and alternate them on the dish with thin slices of skinned melon or figs.

Antipasto di bignè
Savoury Profiteroles

Makes 24

For the filling
1 tablespoon cornflour   25g (1 oz) butter
200ml (7 fl oz) milk   50g (2 oz) ham, diced
a pinch of salt

Make the *bignè* as for sweet *bignè* (page 277).

Make a white sauce: mix the cornflour in a saucepan with a little of the milk until dissolved, add the remaining milk and salt. Stir over moderate heat, until the sauce starts to thicken, then add the butter and remove from the heat. Leave it to cool, stirring from time to time, so a skin does not form on top. Add the ham to the cold sauce. When it is completely cold, fill the *bignè* with a piping bag fitted with a plain nozzle, or a teaspoon.

Pizzetta al prosciutto cotto
Italian Ham Pie

Serves 6

225g (8 oz) self-raising
  flour
75g (3 oz) soft margarine
salt
50ml (2 fl oz) water
3 eggs

150g (5 oz) mild Cheddar
  cheese, grated
100g (4 oz) ham, diced
150ml (¼ pint) double
  cream

Make a pastry by mixing together the flour, margarine and salt until the mixture resembles fine breadcrumbs. Add some of the water, a very little at a time, enough to make it into a soft dough. Mix well, and roll it a few times with the help of a little flour if necessary. Chill for 15 minutes. Grease a 5 ×23cm (2 × 9 inch) ovenproof dish. Roll out the pastry on a lightly floured surface into a circle and line the bottom and sides of the dish. To make the filling, beat the eggs well and mix together with the cheese and ham. Mix in the cream. Pour this mixture into the pastry case and cook in a preheated oven for about 45 minutes at 180°C (350°F), gas mark 4.

Antipasto misto
Mixed Appetizers

Artichokes preserved in olive oil, sold in jars, come in two sizes. The smaller ones are the best. You can also buy tinned artichokes which have been boiled. If you use these, drain them well, mop up any surplus liquid and pour a little olive oil over them. The best oil is the type called 'Vergine', which is the oil that drips from very ripe olives, without even having to be squeezed. Leave covered for 1 hour before use, then use in the same way as artichokes in jars.

You can use tinned anchovies which are already filleted, but, if possible, I suggest you buy the ones called *acciughe salate* (salted anchovies) from an Italian shop. They are pressed in a big tub, deep in salt, and you buy them by the weight. Scrape off the salt or, even better, put one at a time under the cold tap while you brush off the salt with your fingers. Mop up the moisture with a kitchen towel. Remove the bones by pulling apart the two halves of the fish. Lay the fillets on a plate and sprinkle a few drops of olive oil on them. They have a much nicer flavour than the tinned variety.

Serves 6–8

8 artichokes preserved in olive oil
100g (4 oz) anchovies or 140g (5 oz) tin anchovy fillets, drained
8 slices buttered brown bread, cut into thin slices

capers
green and black olives
100g (4 oz) salame casalingo or milanese
100g (4 oz) mortadella
100g (4 oz) capocollo
100g (4 oz) Parma ham
100g (4 oz) best salame

Lift the artichokes out of the jar letting the surplus oil drip back. Cut each artichoke into quarters and arrange on a platter around the edge. Place the anchovy fillets on small strips of sliced buttered bread with one or two capers on top. Use these, together with the green and black olives, to decorate your dish. Fill the middle of the dish with the salted meats. You can also add 2 thinly sliced hardboiled eggs with a rolled anchovy fillet on top of each slice.

Crostini alle acciughe
Toasted Bread with Anchovies

Serves 4

50g (2 oz) butter
1 tablespoon anchovy
   paste
6 slices brown bread

1 tinned red pepper, thinly
   sliced
black and green olives

Soften the butter (take it out of the fridge earlier) and work it a little with a fork. When soft and easy to spread, mix it with the anchovy paste. Cut each slice of bread into two triangles, and toast under the grill on one side only. Spread the anchovy mixture on the toast. Cut the pepper into thin strips. Put one strip on top of each piece of toast together with half an olive. Arrange the toast on a serving dish, with black and green olives between the pieces.

Black olives are a good accompaniment to any *antipasto* or cold snack, but I think they need a little 'doctoring' to make them really tasty. Put them in a colander, rinse under cold water, then drain well. Mop up any moisture with a paper towel. Mix 450g (1 lb) olives with 2 tablespoons of olive oil, so they are well coated, and sprinkle with a generous amount of dried fennel flowers. Mix well, cover and leave in the refrigerator for two hours before using. Keep them stored in the refrigerator.

Instead of fennel flowers, you can use chopped orange rind, cut very thinly. Another alternative is to mix the olives with chopped fresh garlic leaves and basil.

Tartine salate
Savoury Toasts

Serves 4

6 large slices brown bread
3 hardboiled eggs
140g (5 oz) tin anchovy
   fillets
1 dozen stuffed olives
184g (6½ oz) tin tuna

6 artichokes preserved in oil
   (see page 57)
1 tinned yellow or red
   pepper
50g (2 oz) butter
a few capers

Cut away the crusts of the bread with a sharp knife, then cut each slice into 4 triangular or square shapes. Slice the eggs with an egg slicer. Prepare the anchovy fillets by cutting them into small strips. Cut the olives in half. Drain and flake the tuna. Remove the artichokes from the oil and cut into thin slices, then do the same with the pepper. Keep all the ingredients separate.

Melt the butter by placing it in a basin which is standing in a pan of boiling water. With a fork, dip each piece of bread into the butter, so that the butter coats one side only. Place the bread on the grill pan and toast until golden. Arrange some of the anchovies, olives, tuna, artichokes, pepper and capers on top of each one of the pieces of toast. They can look very attractive with a little imagination.

You can use some mayonnaise to decorate them, using the smallest nozzle from an icing set, or by making a forcing bag with an envelope: take a white paper envelope, ordinary letter size, push a couple of spoons of mayonnaise into one of the closed corners, then cut the point with a pair of scissors and, with your hands, screw up the other end of the envelope so the sauce gets pushed through the hole in the corner. I use Hellmann's mayonnaise if I am short of time, but when I can, I make my own as follows:

MAYONNAISE

1 egg yolk
a pinch of salt

100ml (3½ fl oz) olive oil
1 tablespoon vinegar

Place the yolk in a basin with the salt. Using a fork or a hand whisk (not an electric one because you must work slowly), and mixing constantly, add a little oil, drop by drop. Mixing slowly is the secret of well-made mayonnaise. As you add oil, the mayonnaise will thicken. When it gets too thick, add a few drops of vinegar, then add more oil until it is all used. Use the rest of the vinegar at the end to achieve the right consistency. Refrigerate until ready to use.

LEMON MAYONNAISE

Make the sauce as above, adding the juice of 1 lemon, 1 tablespoon chopped parsley, 1 tablespoon finely chopped onions and a few chopped capers. Mix well and keep in the refrigerator. Serve with any cold dish.

Crostini ai fegatini
Chicken Liver Toast Fingers

Take extra care when cleaning the chicken livers, making sure you remove any part which has come into contact with the bile. If any part of the livers shows a discoloured yellowish patch, cut that bit off. It means that in the process of drawing the chicken entrails the bag containing the bile was perforated and the liquid has spilt on to the liver. Those parts will taste very bitter.

Serves 4

4 anchovy fillets, chopped
1 medium-sized onion,
  finely sliced
25g (1 oz) butter
6 chicken livers, any
  membrane removed and
  chopped
250ml (8 fl oz) white wine

1 level tablespoon plain
  flour
freshly ground black
  pepper
salt (optional)
6 slices bread
chopped fresh parsley

Sauté the anchovies and onion in the butter in a small pan, and when the onion is soft, add the livers. Cook for 2 minutes, add the wine and cook for another 5 minutes. Mix the flour into a paste with 1 tablespoon of water, trying to avoid making lumps. Add it to the frying pan, mixing very quickly and constantly. The mixture will thicken. Season with pepper but taste it before putting any salt in. Often when you use anchovies you do not need any more salt. Remove the pan from the heat.

Cut the bread in triangular or rectangular shapes, toast and spread with the mixture. Serve at once, sprinkled with parsley.

Pâté di tonno
Tuna Pâté

Serves 4

100g (4 oz) butter, at room
  temperature
2 hardboiled eggs

184g (6½ oz) tin tuna,
  drained
juice of 1 lemon

Take the butter out of the fridge and let it get soft. When ready, work it with a wooden spoon until creamy. Cool the eggs under the cold tap, then peel them and let them get completely cold. Chop the eggs, flake the tuna, and mash with a fork until they become a paste. Add the creamed butter to the egg mixture with the lemon juice. Beat until well blended. Chill until ready to use.

Antipasto in gelatina
Antipasto in Aspic Jelly

Serves 6

24g (0.85 oz) packet aspic jelly
1 tablespoon vinegar
2 hardboiled eggs, thinly sliced
450g (1 lb) packet frozen or fresh mixed vegetables (see method)
340g (12 oz) tin asparagus
2 tablespoons mayonnaise, plus extra to decorate
184g (6½ oz) tin tuna, drained and flaked

115g (4 oz) tin cocktail sausages, drained and diced
190g (6.6 oz) tin prawns
2 slices of ham, diced
12 green olives, stoned and halved
12 black olives, stoned and halved
12 capers

Dissolve the aspic jelly in 2 tablespoons of cold water, then add enough boiling water to make up 500ml (18 fl oz) liquid. Stir until the jelly is dissolved, then add the vinegar. Leave to cool, but do not let it set. Meanwhile, prepare the rest of the ingredients. If using fresh vegetables, wash and boil separately until tender, then drain, add salt and cut into small pieces. The following vegetables are suitable: green beans, cauliflower, peas, asparagus, carrots, celery, fennel and artichokes. If you use frozen vegetables as I suggest, it saves a lot of time and the result is just as good. Boil the vegetables according to the instructions on the packet, drain and cut into small pieces. All the ingredients must be left to cool. When really cold, mix in two tablespoons of mayonnaise and stir gently to coat evenly. Put them aside. It is very important that all the ingredients are completely cold or the mayonnaise will melt and spoil the effect of the various ingredients showing through the clear, transparent jelly. Some people call this dish 'on the mirror'.

Wet the bottom of an ovenproof dish (6cm/2½ inches deep) and tip the water out. Pour in a few tablespoons of the cold gelatine, tilt to cover the base, then place the dish in the refrigerator until the jelly is set. Arrange the first layer, using all the ingredients to make a decorative pattern. Cover with more gelatine and return to the refrigerator to set. Continue in the same way until you have used up all the ingredients. Put the dish in the refrigerator overnight or for a few hours before serving it to make sure it is well set.

To serve, turn out on to a serving dish and decorate by piping swirls of mayonnaise (see page 61) around its base. (If it does not turn out easily, stand the dish for a few seconds in a bowl with hot water, then invert on to the serving platter.) Serve with crusty bread, brown bread and butter or toast. The Italian way is with crusty bread, as Italians never serve bread and butter.

Antipasto ricco
Rich Appetizer

Serves 6

6 round tomatoes
6 hardboiled eggs, halved
a few radishes
1 lettuce

2 125g (4.41 oz) tins
    sardines, drained
1 tablespoon capers
mayonnaise

Cut the tomatoes in half and remove the seeds and core from the middle, to make hollow bowls. Place an egg half in each tomato half. Scrape, wash and cut the heads of the radishes in 4 sections, leaving a couple of inches of the leafy part showing if possible. Wash and drain the lettuce, removing the leaves at the base, and make a bed of leaves on a serving dish. Arrange the stuffed tomatoes, sardines and the radishes. Decorate with the capers and piped mayonnaise.

Budino di salmone
Salmon Mousse

This mousse can also be made with tinned tuna, or with leftover fresh salmon. Use the leftover egg yolk to make mayonnaise (page 61).

Serves 4

213g (7½ oz) tin salmon,
drained

4 anchovy fillets, drained if
tinned

3 tablespoons fresh white
breadcrumbs

2 tablespoons grated
Parmesan cheese

freshly ground black pepper
(optional)

1 egg

1 egg white

lemon wedges

chopped parsley or parsley
sprigs

mayonnaise

Chop the salmon very finely, together with the anchovy fillets. When it looks like a smooth paste add the breadcrumbs and Parmesan and season. Lightly beat together the egg and egg white, then add to the salmon mixture, mixing well to bind. Take a clean cloth, wet it and squeeze the surplus water out. With your hands, shape the salmon mixture like a large sausage and wrap it in the wet cloth. Twist the ends and tie with cotton. Place it in a saucepan, cover with water and bring it slowly to the boil. Simmer for 45 minutes. Remove it from the water, leave it to cool for about 10 minutes, then remove the cloth and leave the mousse to cool completely. Cut into slices with a very sharp knife. Arrange on a serving dish and decorate with lemon wedges, fresh parsley and some mayonnaise. Serve it with mayonnaise and crusty or sliced brown bread.

Antipasto di vongole
Cockle Appetizer

Serves 4

1kg (2 lb) cockles   *1 lemon*

Clean and scrape the cockles. Rinse them several times until no sand is left. Place them in a large saucepan over a low heat and cover. Shake the pan occasionally and as soon as the cockles open, take them out and keep them hot. Any cockle that does not open *must* be thrown away. Serve them at once, squeezing lemon juice on top. Crusty bread or brown bread are equally suitable to accompany them.

Antipasto ai frutti di mare
Seafood Antipasto

Serves 6

1.5kg (3 lb) mussels
1 clove garlic
1 medium-sized onion,
  peeled and sliced
2 tablespoons olive oil

½ wineglass white wine
1 tablespoon chopped fresh
  parsley
fresh white breadcrumbs

Scrape the mussels well with the blade of a knife, cut off the 'beard' and rinse them well several times, until you are sure you have removed all the grit and sand from the crevices. Put them in a large frying pan over a moderate heat and cover. Shake the pan occasionally. As the mussels open, take them out and put them aside until they are all open. Throw away any that do not open. Discard the half of every shell which is empty. Do not throw away the cooking liquid. Arrange the mussels in their shells on a flameproof dish.

In a frying pan, place the garlic and onion with the olive oil and fry quickly. When the garlic is changing colour, add the wine and boil for a few moments. Remove the garlic, then add 120ml (4 fl oz) of the cooking liquid from the mussels and the chopped parsley. Boil for 3–4 minutes or until the amount of liquid is reduced to half. Spoon a little of this on top of each mussel. Using a teaspoon spread some breadcrumbs on top of each mussel and place the dish under a hot grill to brown for 3–4 minutes. With a fish slice, transfer the mussels on to a serving dish. Serve at once with brown bread or crusty white.

Insalata di riso
Rice Salad

This dish can be used either as an *antipasto* or to accompany any cold dish.

It may be of interest to know that there is always a debate going on in Italian households: 'To wash or not to wash the rice?' It all springs from the fact that before and during the Second World War there was propaganda in favour of not washing rice: 'All the goodness and nourishment will be washed away', or 'Starch is good for you', and so on. The real hidden reason was that Italy was going through a bad patch, with the sanctions imposed on us because of Mussolini's aspiration to a 'place in the sun', so any new practice that would stretch our precarious food supply and help to fill us up was more than welcome and drummed into our ears, until anybody who washed rice felt like a traitor to the motherland.

Serves 6

2 hardboiled eggs
1 tinned red pepper
50g (1¾ oz) tin anchovies,
  drained with oil reserved
184g (6½ oz) tin tuna,
  drained with oil reserved
50g (2 oz) black or green
  olives, stoned

450g (1 lb) long-grain rice
2 tablespoons olive oil
salt
freshly ground black
  pepper
2 tablespoons French
  mustard
a few capers

Chop together the eggs, the pepper, the anchovies, the tuna and the olives. Clean the rice and pick out any grains that look dark in colour. Wash it, changing the water several times to get rid of the excess starch. Put it in a saucepan with 2.5cm (1 inch) water above the level of the rice. Bring it to the boil, then lower the heat, cover and let it simmer for about 15 minutes until tender. Drain in a colander, and rinse under the cold tap to cool it down. Drain thoroughly. Place the rice in a large dish and toss with the olive oil, so the grains will not stick. Season, mix very well, then let it cool down completely. When cold, add the French mustard, and when this is uniformly mixed, add all the remaining ingredients together with the anchovy and tuna oil. Stir well. You can also add small sections of preserved artichokes, any leftover pieces of cold chicken, flakes of cold salmon or other chopped meat or fish.

Coppe di riso
Rice Cups

Serves 4–5 (about 18 'cups')

225g (8 oz) self-raising
  flour
75g (3 oz) margarine
50ml (2 fl oz) water
100g (4 oz) long-grain rice
a pinch of saffron
salt
freshly ground black
  pepper

2 tablespoons olive oil
2 teaspoons capers
2 tablespoons mayonnaise,
  and extra for decorating
chopped fresh parsley
1 slice of ham, diced
100g (4 oz) stuffed olives

Make the pastry by mixing the flour with the margarine, until the mixture resembles fine breadcrumbs, then add the water. Chill for 15 minutes. Roll the pastry, fold over a few times, sprinkling with a little flour, then roll it out to the thickness of about 3mm (⅛ inch). Grease a baking tin. Cut the pastry with a circular cutter or a glass rim and cover the bottom and sides of the tin. Push the pastry well down, then prick it at the bottom with a fork. This is to prevent it rising in the middle of the cups. Bake these cups in a preheated oven for 20 minutes at 210°C (425°F), gas mark 7. When cooked, take the cups out and place them on a wire rack to cool down.

Wash the rice and put in a saucepan with water 5cm (2 inches) above the rice, then add the saffron. Bring it to the boil and simmer for about 15 minutes or until the rice is tender. Drain and tip it into a dish to cool completely. Season. When cold, mix in the olive oil, capers, mayonnaise, parsley and ham. Fill the pastry cups using a teaspoon and on top of each one place a stuffed olive.

Arrange the cups on a serving dish and decorate with a little mayonnaise.

Uova a sorpresa
Surprise Eggs

The following dishes are made with hardboiled eggs that have had the yolks removed and are stuffed in special ways.

UOVA CON SCAMPI   *Eggs with Prawns*

Serves 4

6 *hardboiled eggs*
184g *(6½ oz) tin prawns*

a few capers
mayonnaise to decorate

Cut the eggs in half and remove the yolks, making a clean cut. Drain the prawns and chop half of them into small pieces, then mix them well with the yolks. Fill each egg half with this mixture. Put a whole prawn on top with a couple of capers. Arrange the egg halves in a dish, decorating each with a little mayonnaise.

UOVA CON ACCIUGHE   *Eggs with Anchovies*

Serves 4

6 *hardboiled eggs*
50g *(2 oz) butter*
4 *anchovy fillets, finely*
   chopped

2 *tablespoons mayonnaise*
4 *slices of bread*

Cut the eggs in half and remove the yolks. Then mash the yolks with a fork, adding the butter. When these two ingredients are well blended, add the anchovies. Mix well and add 2 tablespoons of mayonnaise. Fill the egg whites with this mixture (there will be some left over). Cut each slice of bread into two triangles. Toast them one side only and spread the toasted side with the leftover mixture.

UOVA CON SALMONE   *Eggs with Salmon*

Use leftover salmon if you have any.

Serves 4

6 hardboiled eggs	2 teaspoons capers
112g (4½ oz) tin salmon, drained	2 tablespoons mayonnaise
a few lettuce leaves, washed and dried	1 tablespoon parsley, chopped
12 small, whole, pickled onions	

Cut the eggs in half and remove the yolks. Finely chop the salmon, then mix it with the yolks to form a paste, and use to fill the egg whites. Arrange the eggs on a serving dish on a bed of lettuce leaves. Mix the onions and capers with the mayonnaise and place them in the middle of the dish. Decorate with parsley. If there is any of the salmon mixture left, spoon it out here and there as you please.

Giardiniera di verdura
Mixed Pickled Vegetables

These are preserved vegetables that you buy in jars; you can choose mushrooms, baby marrows, green, yellow and red peppers, carrots, artichokes, aubergines and cucumbers, for example. They are first scalded in vinegar, then sealed in jars, covered with olive oil. The strong vinegar taste is modified, and the vegetables have just a trace of piquancy. They are a very useful accompaniment to ham and *salame* as a winter *antipasto*, or they can be served together with any dish when fresh vegetables are scarce. You can take a little at a time from a jar and the rest will keep, as long as you top up with more oil.

Carciofi lessati
Boiled Artichokes

Serves 4

1 globe artichoke per person
2 lemons or juice of 1 lemon and a few drops of vinegar

salt
½ teaspoon butter per artichoke, or a little olive oil and lemon juice, or mayonnaise

Always choose fresh, compact, green artichokes. Trim the stems level with the leaves, but do not throw the stems away. Prepare a large bowl of cold water with some lemon juice or a few drops of vinegar. Discard the outside leaves of the globes, but not too many, then proceed to trim the top of the leaves (cut off about ½cm/¼ inch) with a very sharp knife. Shake the artichokes with your fingers so they will open a little. Wash well, then place them in the bowl of water, one at a time, so they will not discolour. Rinse them well, drain and arrange in a saucepan, heads down, with water to cover. Add salt and the juice of one lemon. Boil them for 5 minutes, then reduce the heat and let them simmer for about 45 minutes, until tender. Try one of the outside leaves, to check if they're done. If the base is cooked they are ready. Drain well, place them in individual dishes, and put in the middle of each one a knob of butter, if you serve them hot. If you prefer them cold, leave them to cool and serve with a little olive oil and lemon juice or mayonnaise.

To eat globe artichokes, detach each leaf with your fingers, eating the tender part at the base. As you get nearer to the heart, the leaves will be tender all over and you can eat the lot. The stems are also edible. Peel them, cut into sections and proceed in the same way as for the leaves.

Instead of serving artichokes whole, you can quarter them before boiling, in which case you will have to discard all the outer leaves before cooking.

Pinzimonio
Crudité Sauce

Pinzimonio is a sauce for raw vegetables.

Serves 4

2 *hearts of celery*
6 *medium-sized or 4 large
  carrots*
2 *fennels*
8 *radishes*

8 *tablespoons olive oil*
salt
*freshly ground black
  pepper*

74

Cut the celery stems at the base, scrape and wash them. Cut the stems into sections, and then into thin strips. Scrape and wash the carrots and cut them into strips. Clean the fennels, discarding the outside leaf, then divide them into 8 sections each, and wash. Scrape the radishes and cut them into quarters, then wash them. Rinse all the vegetables well and drain.

Use one saucer per person. In each saucer mix 2 tablespoons olive oil, 1 teaspoon salt and ½ teaspoon black pepper. Dip the strips of raw vegetables into this mixture as you eat them with crusty bread and mop up with some bread any leftover sauce.

Pane all'aglio
Garlic Bread

The best type of bread for this purpose is a crisp white loaf. Cut some slices and toast them on both sides. Rub a clove of garlic on the toast and sprinkle it with a little of the best olive oil. Wrap a napkin around to keep it hot. Serve at once.

Olive e olio d'oliva
Olives and Olive Oil

Olives grow in many parts of central and southern Italy and are indispensable in the preparation of *antipasti*. In many homes they are preserved in very big earthenware jars. The trees do not withstand severe winters, and are very precious to their owners: an olive tree takes twelve years to bear fruit, and can live for hundreds of years. It is said that the olive trees on the Mount of Olives, under which Jesus used to sit and talk to his disciples, still grow. In the olive groves the trees are never planted near one another, and you will never find an olive tree with a straight trunk, without holes and niches. A legend says that this is because the devil, in a fit of temper, hit them very hard with his horns as he was trying to hide in an olive grove and found that it was impossible to do so because the trees were too far apart.

Olive oil is used in the home in many ways, not only for cooking. A little of it on a piece of bread, with pepper and salt, makes a very tasty open sandwich which Italians call *panzanella*. It is good for your hair, warmed up and rubbed into the scalp, and for your skin – a small amount in a piece of cotton wool will help to soften roughness on elbows and heels – and equal parts of olive oil and water, well beaten together, will bring relief to sunburn. There is no end to its uses and usefulness.

During the war my brother swallowed a nail, and there was not a doctor for miles around. It was only thanks to my mother putting him on a diet of bread soaked in olive oil that he escaped from this mishap in good health.

Olive farcite
Stuffed Olives

Stuffed olives are very expensive, so if you can spare the time why not prepare them at home? You only need a little patience. Take a very sharp, pointed knife and peel off the olives from their stone, in a continuous circular motion, rather like when you peel an orange. In this way you can take the stones out and then roll back the olives to look whole again. Chop up one preserved red pepper, one pimento, some capers, a couple of anchovy fillets, a gherkin and a preserved artichoke, or anything else you may like to use. Fill each olive with some of the bits you have prepared.

Arance e olive nere
Oranges and Black Olives

Serves 4

4 large oranges	freshly ground black
100g (4 oz) black olives	pepper
2 tablespoons olive oil	salt

Peel and slice the oranges, removing the pith, then cut them into small sections. Wash the olives in a colander under the cold tap. Drain them well and dry with a paper towel. Mix together the olives and oranges, and place in a bowl. Pour over the olive oil, add pepper and a very little salt. Mix well, and serve with crusty bread.

Arance alla griglia
Grilled Oranges

1 orange per person	olive oil
sugar or salt	

Peel the oranges, removing the pith, and cut them into slices ½cm (¼ inch) thick. Arrange the slices on an enamel plate and sprinkle them with a little sugar and a few drops of olive oil. Place the plate under a hot grill for a few minutes, until the sugar is all dissolved, then serve at once while they are still very hot.

Some people prefer to sprinkle the slices with salt instead of sugar. Try both ways and see which you like best. Either way they are delicious, as an appetizer, for a quick snack or with any cold dish.

'Becche' (semi di zucca)
Marrow Seeds

The name *becche* is slang for marrow seeds which have been roasted and salted. You can see them on sale in kiosks, at football matches, parks and cinemas, and there are still streetsellers who will carry a huge sack of them across their shoulder and sell them along the road in small cartons. I know one of these vendors who shouts '*Passatempi*' (time fillers) to advertise his merchandise of *becche*, *lupini* (lupins) and *nocciole* (monkey nuts).

To make *becche* you need a big, ripe, yellow marrow. It must be very ripe so that the seeds are fully developed. If it is really ripe, when you cut the marrow in half the seeds will not stick to any part of the flesh but come out clean and dry. Cut the marrow and take all the seeds out. Wash them well getting rid of any bits of membrane, until they do not feel slimy any more. Drain them and mop the surplus water with a piece of kitchen paper, but leave them a little damp. Sprinkle them with fine table salt until they are well coated with it. Put them on a baking tray, one layer only, and place the tray in a hot oven for about 15 minutes. They must not roast, but they will be ready as they start to change colour. Leave them to cool.

The secret of opening the seeds easily, to take the inside of the seed out to eat, is to hold them by the rounded part and put the pointed part between your front teeth. Put a small amount of pressure on the point (vertically) and the seed will crack open in no time.

Lupini
Lupins

Lupins are a type of pulse but are not cooked like the others because they are not very nutritious. Their plants grow quite tall, with big seed pods which will dry in the sun before harvesting. If you walk through them they will jingle like bells. A legend says that it was because of this that they were cursed by the Virgin Mary. During the flight into Egypt, Mary took refuge in a field of lupins which were ready to be harvested to avoid the soldiers who were pursuing her. The pods were making a lot of noise as she crouched in the middle of them, and fearing the soldiers would hear, Mary turned to the plants and cursed them, saying, 'You will be of no use to anybody.' So it is that, no matter how many lupins you eat, you will never feel satisfied, which explains the uselessness of the plant and why they are called just '*passatempi*'.

2

Minestre, Risotti e Gnocchi

Soups, Risotto and Gnocchi

Italians are very fond of soups: in nearly all the homes in the morning there will be a tall saucepan simmering either with meat broth or vegetable broth or minestrone, to be ready by lunchtime. Nearly all Italian working men go home in the middle of the day for their lunch, as well as the children who do not have afternoon school, so the housewife has the task of preparing a meal at midday. Meat broth is strained, and some small kind of pasta cooked in it, while the meat, *bollito*, will be the second course, accompanied by some seasonal vegetables or by a *giardiniera* of preserved ones in the winter. Some families, who have to stretch their budget, will probably have cheese after the soup or *salame* or ham, leaving the meat from the broth for their evening meal. It will probably be served with some sauce, together with potatoes or other vegetables and bread.

Soup plates vary a lot in size: Italian ones are much bigger than the soup bowls you buy in England, for example. But I always count two ladles (340ml/11 fl oz) per person, which seems to be about the right amount.

Bought Pasta

There are so many shapes and sizes of pasta for soups or for *pastasciutta*, which literally means 'dry pasta', and describes any pasta drained and served with a sauce, in contrast to a pasta dish with liquid in it, like a soup. Leaving aside the homemade pasta (see pages 144–5), pasta bought by the kilogram comes in many different shapes and is referred to by many different names. The best type to look for when you buy it are the pasta *all'uovo* (made with eggs) which are not completely smooth but have little ridges on them.

I have only noted the names that translate easily (see pages 82–3), because you will find that the names of a good many pasta types come from southern dialect (wheat is extensively cultivated in the south, and hence most of the pasta factories are there), and these are untranslatable!

Croutons

You need the bread to be at least one day old. Cut slices of about 1cm (½ inch) thick, take off the crust, cut the slices into strips about 1cm (½ inch) wide, then cut these

Pasta shapes for serving with a sauce (*pastasciutta*)

Capelli d'angelo
Angel's hair

Tagliatelle

Rigatoni
(*sections like tubing, with ridges*)

Ditali
Thimbles

Fusilli
Twists

Cannolicchi
(*similar to rigatoni*)

Penne
Feathers

Mezze penne

Tubetti
Little tubes

Smaller pasta shapes to use in soups

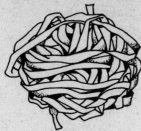

Millerighe
A thousand lines

Farfalline
Little butterflies

Semi melone
Melon seeds

Stelline
Little stars

Perline
Little pearls

Quadretti
Squares

Orzo
Barley

Anellini
Little rings

Conchiglie
Shells

Lumachine
Little snails

Peperini
Little peppercorns

into squares. If you like, you can cut the bread into fancy shapes. The croutons may be fried in boiling oil or soaked in stock and browned on a greased tin in a hot oven. They should be golden in colour. If fried, place them on some kitchen paper to drain well after cooking.

Brodo di manzo
Beef Broth

This broth is the basis of many Italian soups. The secret of a good tasty broth is to add the salt first and bring to the boil very slowly.

Serves 4

450g (1 lb) stewing beef, trimmed and cut into 2.5cm (1 inch) cubes
2 litres (4 pints) water
salt
1 medium-sized tomato, halved

1 medium-sized carrot, chopped
1 stick celery, chopped
1 medium-sized onion, sliced

Place the meat in a saucepan with the water and some salt. Very slowly heat and bring it to the boil. Add the tomato, carrot, celery and onion. Let it simmer for about 3 hours, using a slotted spoon to remove any scum from the surface.

When the broth is ready, lift out the pieces of meat, put them in a basin with one ladle of the liquid, then cover it and keep it hot. Strain the broth. If you want it to be clear, do not squash the vegetables, but it's up to you. It should not be too fatty, because you will have trimmed any fat off the meat. Adjust the amount if necessary by adding more water and salt if the liquid has reduced too much during boiling.

Brodo di cappone
Capon Broth

When I think of capons my mind goes back to a hot Italian summer's day, the day of the making of capons. The figure of an old woman who came to my grandmother's farm sometime in July has stuck in my memory since I was a child. We used to call her 'the witch'. She was fat with long grey hair piled high on the top of her head and she wore on the top a black scarf knotted at the nape of her neck. She was considered a sort of visiting witch who, by her magic powers, would change the cockerels into capons. It would be possible to sleep in peace after she had taken away their power of crowing, and our early mornings would be disturbed no more by their almost continuous *chicchirichi*.

The woman had very fat, greasy hands, and a similarly greasy smile which would make us children shiver with fright in case we incurred her displeasure. We did not understand then that her magic powers lay in her basket, in the shape of a pair of sharp scissors, a needle and thread.

She would sit on a stool under a shady tree. The cockerels would be gathered, their legs tied with a piece of tape, and they would be waiting at her feet for the treatment which they would receive one by one, after which they would be set free, unable to move for a while, then would start jerking until they got enough strength to hop to a spot in the shade to recover, while the woman was left with a plateful of testicles and combs. (These are a great delicacy made into a sort of pâté spread on fresh bread. I do not think I will bother to give you the recipe!) To me, then, a mere seven-year-old, this was the height of witchcraft.

Serves 6–7

1 capon, about 2kg (4 lb)   1 medium-sized onion,
salt   sliced
2.75 litres (5 pints) water   1 carrot, chopped
1 tomato quartered   4 basil leaves
1 stick celery, chopped

Clean the capon, washing it well inside and out. You can please yourself as to whether you cut it in quarters or leave it whole. Place the capon in a large saucepan over moderate heat with salt and the water. Heat it slowly and bring to the boil, then add the vegetables. Cover and simmer for about 3 hours, very slowly. Add more water and salt if necessary. When the broth is ready, lift the capon out and keep it hot until ready to serve. Strain the broth and use it to cook cappelletti (see page 157).

Minestra con frattaglie di pollo
Chicken Giblet Soup

This soup can be made with capon, chicken or turkey broth. When making the broth as described above, include the bird's giblets (gizzard, liver and heart). When the broth is cooked, remove the giblets and cut them into very small pieces, then return to the strained broth.

With this soup, homemade fresh quadretti are a must. You need 300ml (½ pint) of broth and 65g (2½ oz) of pasta per serving.

If you would like to try this soup and do not have chicken broth available, buy some giblets and proceed as follows:

Serves 4

2 sets chicken giblets
1.75 litres (3 pints) water
2½ chicken stock cubes
1 medium-sized carrot
1 medium-sized onion
1 tomato

1 stick celery
2 basil leaves
homemade pasta (page 144)
grated Parmesan cheese, to serve

Clean the giblets (pull the inner skin off the gizzards) and wash them all well. Make the broth in the same way as the capon broth above. Cook the quadretti in the strained broth adding the small pieces of giblets. Serve with grated Parmesan.

Riso e piselli
Thick Rice and Pea Soup

Serves 4

275g (10 oz) rice (any type, but Italian recommended)
4 rashers rindless unsmoked bacon, diced
75g (3 oz) margarine
a pinch of fresh chopped basil

450g (1 lb) fresh peas, shelled
salt
1 litre (1¾ pints) water
1 beef stock cube
grated Parmesan cheese, to serve

Wash the rice. Place the bacon in a large saucepan and heat it very slowly so that the fat melts. Add the margarine and the basil, then after a few minutes add the peas and the rice and season. Stir from time to time, until the peas are tender. Dissolve the stock cube in the water and add to the rice. Bring it to the boil and simmer for about 15 minutes or until the rice is tender. Add more salt if necessary. Serve with Parmesan cheese.

Stracciatella
Egg Soup

Stracciatella is an exquisite soup, and very quick to make. It is best made with beef or chicken broth, but as a last resort it can also be made with stock cubes. This soup also has the advantage of not spoiling if not served at once. You can leave it and reheat it without the soup losing its flavour or consistency.

Serves 4

2 *eggs*
salt
*a pinch of ground
  cinnamon*
3 *tablespoons fresh white
  breadcrumbs*

3 *tablespoons grated
  Parmesan cheese*
1.25 *litres (2¼ pints) beef or
  chicken broth (page 84),
  or 3 stock cubes dissolved
  in water*

Beat the eggs well, add salt and pepper, the cinnamon, breadcrumbs and the Parmesan cheese. Mix very well, while bringing the broth to the boil. Take one ladle of the broth from the pan and mix it with the mixture, stirring well. Tip this back into the boiling broth, stirring continuously for about 1 minute, while it boils. Serve at once, with croutons (page 81), toast or just as it is.

Riso all'uovo
Thick Rice and Egg Soup

Serves 4

400g (15 oz) rice
salt
water
2 eggs

2 teaspoons butter
4 tablespoons grated
Parmesan cheese

Wash the rice. Put it in a large saucepan, with the salt, and enough water to come about 3cm (1½ inches) above the rice. When it comes to the boil, lower the heat, cover, and let it simmer for about 15–20 minutes until tender. By then there should be hardly any water left, but the rice should not be too dry either; it should look like a thick soup, so adjust with a little water if necessary. If you have added any water, bring it to the boil again. Beat the eggs, season and add them to the rice, mixing quickly, then remove the pan from the heat at once. Add the butter, stirring constantly to mix. Serve in soup plates, with 1 tablespoon of grated Parmesan on top of each portion.

Minestra di ceci
Chickpea Soup

Serves 4

450g (1 lb) chickpeas	1 sprig of rosemary
75ml (3 fl oz) olive oil	4 anchovy fillets, chopped
1 clove garlic	
1 medium-sized onion, chopped	

Rinse the chickpeas, being careful that there are no bits of grit or little stones, then soak them overnight in a basin. (Make sure the basin is about double the size of the amount of beans as by morning their volume will more or less have doubled.) Place 2 tablespoons of the olive oil in a large saucepan over moderate heat and add the garlic, onion, rosemary and anchovy fillets. When the onion is tender, discard the garlic.

Boil the chickpeas in a pressure cooker with salt for the time specified in the instruction manual. Or simmer for 1 hour or more until tender. When the beans are cooked, mix them with the other ingredients, adding more boiling water as necessary to make up enough soup for 4 servings. Serve the soup, mix 1 teaspoon of olive oil into each portion.

Minestrone

A mixture of spinach, beans, courgettes, peas, tomatoes, one small potato, 2 sticks of celery, a little parsley, 2 big carrots, or any other vegetables you like, can be added to make minestrone. I am not giving exact weights for the different types, because you can put in what you have available without being too fussy, as long as you have the right amount when they are all clean.

Serves 4

100g (4 oz) margarine
1kg (2 lb) mixed fresh
  vegetables, washed and
  chopped
salt
freshly ground black
  pepper

1.25 litres (2¼ pints)
  boiling water
toast and grated Parmesan
  cheese, to serve

Melt the margarine in a large saucepan. Add the chopped vegetables, season and cook them very slowly, stirring from time to time. Make sure they do not stick to the pan. When the vegetables are tender, add boiling water to make enough for 4 servings. Serve minestrone with toast and grated Parmesan cheese.

Minestrone passato
Strained Minestrone

Use the same vegetables as in the previous recipe.

Serves 4

100g (4 oz) margarine
1kg (2 lb) mixed fresh
  vegetables, washed and
  chopped
salt
freshly ground black
  pepper

550ml (1 pint) boiling
  water
150ml (¼ pint) double
  cream
grated Parmesan cheese, to
  serve

Make the minestrone as in the previous recipe up to the point where the vegetables are cooked. Remove the vegetables from the pan, and let them cool down a little. Put them in a liquidizer and blend to a smooth purée. Pour this purée into a saucepan, add the boiling water and the double cream. Stir well, bring to the boil, check the seasoning, and serve at once with a little grated cheese sprinkled on top. Remove from the heat as soon as it reaches the boil or the cream may curdle.

Minestra di patate
Potato Soup

Serves 4

100g (4 oz) margarine
4 large potatoes, peeled and cubed
salt
freshly ground black pepper

2 beef stock cubes
225g (8 oz) pasta for soups
grated Parmesan cheese, to serve

Melt the margarine in a saucepan over moderate heat and add the potatoes, salt and pepper. Stir very often, while the potatoes cook slowly. When they are soft, add the stock cubes dissolved in 150ml (¼ pint) boiling water. Bring the soup to the boil again, adding enough water to make 1.25 litres (2¼ pints) liquid. Return to the boil, add the pasta, stirring often, and simmer, stirring frequently, until the pasta is tender. Serve it with grated Parmesan cheese.

Pasta e fagioli
Pasta and Beans

At the end of the summer in Italy, you can buy fresh beans to be shelled which are quick to cook and do not require soaking like dried beans. Their taste is definitely superior and it is a treat to make a soup with them, because they are on sale only for a few days. I have never seen them here, but if you grow French beans in your garden it is worth leaving the last of the crop to use them this way. You leave them on the plant until the pod dries up.

If you do not have time to make homemade pasta (quadretti), substitute packet tagliatelle cut into little squares.

Serves 4

225g (8 oz) homemade
  pasta (page 144)
750g (1½ lb) beans,
  unshelled weight
100g (4 oz) margarine
1 medium-sized onion,
  peeled and chopped

6 fresh basil leaves,
  chopped
salt
2 tomatoes, peeled, seeded
  and chopped
grated Parmesan cheese, to
  serve

Cut up the pasta. Shell the beans and wash them. Melt the margarine in a saucepan over a moderate heat with the onion and basil. Cook it slowly until the onion is soft, then add the beans and salt. Stir and cook for 5 minutes, then add the tomatoes and 50ml (2 fl oz) water. Go on stirring often, until the beans are soft, then add enough water to the soup to make 1.25 litres (2¼ pints). When it boils again, drop in the pasta and cook for 5 minutes. (If you are not using fresh homemade pasta, the cooking time will be quite a bit longer.) Adjust the seasoning, and serve at once with grated Parmesan cheese.

Passatelli
Strained Pasta Soup

Serves 3

900ml (1½ pints) broth or
   stock
1 tablespoon plain flour
3 tablespoons fresh white
   breadcrumbs

2 eggs, beaten
salt
1 tablespoon grated
   Parmesan cheese, to
   serve

Make the broth, not filling the saucepan more than three-quarters full. Mix the flour, breadcrumbs and egg together to make a soft dough. Season with salt. Place the dough, a piece at a time, in a colander with holes about ½cm (¼ inch) in diameter and push it through making little tubes. Cut these into small sections with a sharp knife as they are squeezed through and let them drop into the boiling broth. When you have finished, stir and let boil for 5 minutes. Serve with a little Parmesan.

Riso e fagioli borlotti
Rice and Beans

Serves 6

300g (10 oz) dried beans
4 tablespoons olive oil
4 slices unsmoked streaky
   bacon
1 onion, peeled and
   chopped
1 stick celery, chopped

2 tomatoes, peeled, seeded
   and chopped
a small piece of pimento,
   chopped
salt
450g (1 lb) rice, washed

Clean the beans and remove any which are broken or discoloured. Soak overnight in a large basin, taking into account that the beans will swell to double the original size. Next morning, boil the beans in a pressure cooker for about 10 minutes, then rinse them in hot water and keep hot. Put the oil in a large saucepan over a moderate heat, with the bacon, onion and celery. Stir and cook slowly until the onion is soft and the bacon crisp, then add the beans, tomatoes and pimento and season with salt. Continue simmering for about 20 minutes, adding 1 tumbler of water. Add the rice and ½ litre (18 fl oz) boiling water. Stir and simmer until the rice is cooked (about 15–20 minutes). If it gets too thick, add another ½ tumbler of water. Stir often and do not let the rice stick to the bottom of the pan. This soup should be quite thick, like a risotto, so if you need to add some water to finish cooking the rice, add only ½ tumbler at a time.

Minestra di cipolle
Onion Soup

Serves 6

120g (5 oz) butter
1 large onion, peeled and sliced
2 tablespoons plain flour
1.2 litres (2 pints) water
salt

4 eggs, lightly beaten
6 tablespoons grated Parmesan cheese
freshly ground black pepper
6 slices toast, to serve

Melt the butter in a large saucepan over moderate heat, add the onion and cook for 3–5 minutes until soft. Mix the flour with 2 tablespoons of cold water, making a smooth paste. Boil the remaining water and gradually mix it with the paste and return to the pan, then add salt. Boil for 30 minutes. In a large basin, mix the eggs with the Parmesan, then add the broth to this mixture, a ladle at a time, stirring well. Adjust the seasoning and serve at once with toast.

Minestra di spinaci
Spinach Soup

Serves 4

500g (1 lb) spinach
salt
freshly ground black
  pepper
350ml (12 fl oz) milk
2 beef stock cubes

600ml (1 pint) boiling
  water
a pinch of ground
  cinnamon
2 tablespoons grated
  Parmesan cheese

Clean and wash the spinach well. Drain as well as you can. Cut it up very small, then cook in a saucepan over moderate heat, stirring often until tender. Season. When the water from the spinach has evaporated, add the milk and the cubes dissolved in the boiling water. Mix the cinnamon with the Parmesan and add to the soup. Serve with croutons (page 81) on top.

Minestra di fave
Broad Bean Soup

Serves 4

2 tablespoons olive oil
2 small onions
100g (4 oz) prosciutto,
  chopped
1 tablespoon chopped fresh
  parsley
a pinch of marjoram
2 beef stock cubes
1.2 litres (2 pints) water

1 tablespoon tomato purée
1kg (2 lb) fresh broad beans,
  unshelled
salt
freshly ground black
  pepper
4 slices toast, to serve
grated Parmesan or
  pecorino cheese, to serve

Heat the oil in a large saucepan and add the onions, *prosciutto*, parsley and marjoram. Cook, stirring, until the onions are tender, then dilute the stock cubes in the boiling water and stir in the tomato purée until all dissolved. Add to the saucepan with the beans and simmer until the beans are cooked. Adjust the seasoning if necessary. Line the bottom of the soup plates with the toast and spoon over the soup. Serve with grated Parmesan or *pecorino* cheese.

Minestra di piselli freschi
Fresh Pea Soup

Serves 4

500g (1 lb) fresh peas,
  unshelled
2 basil leaves, chopped
50g (2 oz) butter
2 rashers unsmoked bacon,
  chopped
1 small onion, peeled and
  sliced
salt
freshly ground black
  pepper

1 teaspoon tomato purée
1.1 litres (2 pints) boiling
  water
1 beef stock cube,
  crumbled
225g (8 oz) small shaped
  pasta for soups (page
  83)
grated Parmesan cheese, to
  serve

Rinse the peas and drain them, then mix with the basil. Melt the butter in a saucepan over moderate heat and add the bacon and the finely chopped onion. Fry slowly, until the onion is tender and the bacon is crisp, then add the peas, mix well and season. After about 5 minutes, dilute the tomato purée with a little of the water, add the beef cube, then add to the saucepan with some more water. Stir well to dissolve the beef cube. Keep stirring while the peas cook, adding a little more of the water (about one ladleful), and when soft add the rest of the water. Bring it to the boil and add the pasta of your choice. Simmer until tender, stirring often. Adjust the seasoning and serve with grated Parmesan cheese.

Risotto alla milanese
Milanese Risotto

Serves 4

450g (1 lb) Italian rice
(Arborio)
a piece of beef marrow (the
size of an egg)
1 small onion, peeled and
thinly sliced
100g (4 oz) butter

1.5 litres (2½ pints) beef
stock
a pinch of saffron
50g (2 oz) grated Parmesan
cheese, plus extra for
serving

Wash the rice under cold running water and drain well. Chop the marrow (you can buy a bone for the marrow, and don't worry if it is a smaller piece than I suggest). Put the chopped marrow in a large saucepan over a moderate heat, with the onion and one tablespoon of the butter. Cook slowly until the onion is soft but not browned. In the meantime, bring the stock to the boil. Add the rice to the pan with the onion and mix with a wooden spoon. Pour in a little of the boiling stock and keep stirring. Stir and add more stock as the rice swells. After 6–7 minutes, add the saffron. Keep adding stock until the rice is cooked (15–20 minutes). Add the rest of the butter and mix in the Parmesan. Serve very hot; you may want to add a little more Parmesan on the top.

Risotto con funghi
Mushroom Risotto

Serves 4

65g (2½ oz) margarine
1 small onion, peeled and chopped
1 tablespoon fresh chopped parsley
350g (12 oz) mushrooms, quartered
salt
freshly ground black pepper

2 397g (14 oz) tins Italian tomatoes
1 beef stock cube
100ml (3 fl oz) boiling water
400g (15 oz) Italian rice (Arborio)
grated Parmesan cheese, to serve

Melt the margarine in a large saucepan and fry the onion and parsley for a few minutes until the onion is soft, stirring, then add the mushrooms, salt and pepper. Stir occasionally. Strain the tomatoes, pushing all the pulp through a sieve. Add the tomatoes to the pan and let everything simmer for about ½ hour. Add 1 beef stock cube dissolved in the hot water. Have a kettle of boiling water ready. Add 150ml (¼ pint) hot water, stir and tip in the rice. Bring it to the boil again, stirring almost continuously. Let the rice simmer and cook slowly, while from time to time you add boiling water from the kettle, a little at a time, so the rice will finish cooking without sticking. After about 15 minutes, test the rice to see if it is tender enough. Add more salt, if required. Serve with grated cheese.

Risotto al ragù
Risotto with Meat and Tomato Sauce

Make a *ragù* sauce as on page 146. If you should have some *ragù* in your freezer, take out the right amount and warm it slowly in a saucepan.

Serves 6

600g (20 oz) rice
600ml (1 pint) water
salt
freshly ground black
  pepper

75g (3 oz) grated Parmesan
  cheese

Wash the rice under cold running water and drain well. Put it in a saucepan with enough water to come about 5cm (2 inches) above it. Bring to the boil slowly and simmer for 5–6 minutes. In a separate pan, bring the *ragù* sauce to the boil. Drain the partly cooked rice and add it to the *ragù*, stirring with a wooden spoon. Have some water boiling in a kettle. As you stir the rice, add some of the water and continue adding water until the rice is cooked. Season. Serve your risotto either by putting it all in a large deep dish or in individual portions. Add the Parmesan after the risotto is served or it will stick to the saucepan.

Risotto con spinaci
Thick Spinach and Rice Soup

Serves 6

500g (1 lb) fresh spinach,
  washed and chopped
1.2 litres (2 pints) water
400g (14 oz) rice, rinsed

salt
75g (3 oz) butter
75g (3 oz) grated Parmesan
  cheese, to serve

Place the spinach in a saucepan over a low heat and cook, stirring often until soft and the moisture evaporated. When soft, add the water and the rice. Simmer for about 15 minutes, then taste and add salt. Mix in the butter, then serve on individual plates. Sprinkle the Parmesan over and mix in with each portion.

Gnocchi di patate [Ⓕ]
Gnocchi Made with Potatoes

Gnocchi are small dumplings. In this recipe they are made from potatoes but they can also be made from semolina. You can make different sauces for gnocchi. *Ragù* (meat and tomato) is often used, but a very good sauce is made with stewing lamb. Start the sauce first, then make gnocchi when the sauce is nearly ready. If you are using frozen gnocchi, do not take them out of the freezer until it is time to drop them into the boiling water.

Serves 4

50g (2 oz) margarine
1 onion, peeled and
  chopped
1 stick celery, chopped
1 small carrot, chopped
a few chopped fresh basil
  leaves or a pinch of dry
  basil

450g (1 lb) neck of lamb
salt
2 397g (14 oz) tins Italian
  peeled tomatoes
1 tablespoon tomato purée
260ml (½ pint) water

For the gnocchi
1kg (2 lb) potatoes
225g (8 oz) plain flour

grated pecorino or
  Parmesan cheese

Melt the margarine in a saucepan and add the onion, celery, carrot and basil, stirring until the onion is tender. Add the meat and season. Cook for 5–10 minutes, stirring occasionally. Drain the tomatoes through a sieve, removing the seeds, and add to the pan. Dilute the tomato purée with a little of the water, and pour it in, stirring. Return to the boil, add the rest of the water, cover the pan and let it simmer for about 1½ hours. The sauce should be like a custard, but not too thick, so adjust with a little boiling water if needed while cooking.

To make the gnocchi, boil the potatoes until you can push a fork easily through them. Do not be tempted to peel the potatoes before cooking, because they will be watery, and one of the secrets of good gnocchi is to avoid water in the potatoes. As soon as the potatoes are cooked, drain and peel them. Mash them on a board while still hot, making sure you do not leave any lumps. Add the flour, making a dough which you can knead. Roll out the dough, taking a piece in your hands to make a sausage shape, about 2cm (1 inch) thick. Use flour if necessary to help with the shaping. Flatten each piece and cut into sections about

4cm (1½ inches) long, with a slanting cut. Make two small depressions with your fingers into each one, so that the gnocchi hold their sauce better.

Leave the gnocchi on a floured board and quickly finish the remaining dough in the same way. Have ready a large saucepan with salted water. When the sauce is cooked and the water boiling, add the gnocchi. Return to the boil and cook for 2 minutes, stirring with a wooden spoon from time to time. Lift them out of the water with a slotted spoon, being careful not to break them. Put a couple of spoonfuls of the sauce into individual dishes, followed by a layer of gnocchi, then sprinkle liberally with Parmesan cheese. For gnocchi, grated *pecorino* cheese is used more than Parmesan, but it is up to your preference which one you use. Make a second layer of gnocchi in the same way, without mixing, or they might stick to each other. Share the pieces of lamb on top of each portion: eat the meat together with gnocchi and pick the bones!

To freeze gnocchi, place them on a floured freezer-proof tray. Fill the tray, then place it in the freezer for about ½ hour. When the gnocchi are frozen, pop them in a freezer bag, label, seal and return to the freezer.

Gnocchi alla romana
Gnocchi the Roman Way

The name of this dish is a bit misleading, because the gnocchi do not look at all like ordinary gnocchi. Some people call them 'semolina gnocchi'.

Serves 6

1 litre (1¾ pints) milk
250g (9 oz) semolina
100g (4 oz) butter
2 egg yolks, lightly beaten

175g (6 oz) grated
Parmesan cheese
salt

Heat the milk in a large saucepan over moderate heat. When hot, but not boiling, pour in the semolina, one tablespoon at a time, mixing continuously with a wooden spoon. If any lumps develop, remove the pan from the heat and stir vigorously. Continue stirring, lower the heat and cook for about 10 minutes. The mixture will be quite thick.

Remove from the heat, mix in half of the butter, the egg yolks, 1 tablespoon of Parmesan cheese and salt. Stir everything well together, then tip this mixture on a damp worktop or a board (wet beforehand with a kitchen towel dipped in water). Spread with the blade of a wet palette knife to the thickness of about 1cm (½ inch). Leave to cool for about 1 hour. When cold, cut into 5cm (2 inch) squares. Grease a shallow and wide ovenproof dish, then place the squares in layers, sprinkling grated Parmesan on top of each layer. Do not make more than 3 or 4 layers; if they do not fit in, use another dish. Melt the remaining butter in a small pan, and pour it on top of the last layer of Parmesan. Preheat the oven and bake at 200°C (400°F), gas mark 6, for 15 minutes until golden brown.

Crema di legumi
Cream of Pulses Soup

Pulses are edible seeds growing in pods such as beans, peas, broad beans, chickpeas and lentils. You can use them fresh or dry. Any of the above types are suitable for this soup. If you are using fresh seeds, just shell and wash them. If they are dry, you soak them overnight, except the lentils.

Serves 4

400g (15 oz) fresh shelled or dried pulses
4 basil leaves
1.2 litres (2 pints) water
3 beef stock cubes
50ml (2 fl oz) olive oil

salt
freshly ground black pepper
grated pecorino cheese, to serve

The fresh pulses can be boiled in a saucepan, while the soaked dried pulses must be cooked in a pressure cooker for 10 minutes. When cooked, rinse well in hot water, then blend to a purée in a liquidizer with the basil leaves. Boil the water, use a little to dissolve the stock cubes, then add this to the purée, and mix it with the rest of the water and olive oil. Season and serve, with grated *pecorino* cheese sprinkled over the top.

3

Insalate e Verdure
Salads and Vegetables

Salads

Italians eat a lot of salad, summer or winter, at lunch or dinner. It is nearly always served on its own, but never without a dressing, although it may be served to tourists that way because that is how Italians think they like it. No true Italian would dream of an undressed salad on his own table – fit only for rabbits!

Salad ingredients are always chopped small. In the summer, peppers, tomatoes, cucumbers (the short type), onions and radishes will be included, while in winter chicory, endive, fennel and celery are used. Some people cut up a few leaves from a growing garlic plant to add flavour, but if you like just a hint of garlic, rub your salad bowl with a crushed clove before mixing in the salad.

In Italy they never use ready-made dressings bought in

bottles – but invariably the same sort of ingredients are made up to dress a salad: vinegar and olive oil, lemon juice, salt. An Italian saying goes, 'A salad is perfect when it has a sage to provide the salt, a miser the vinegar, a generous person the olive oil and a madman to mix it!'

Don't mix your salad with the dressing until just before you serve it – or it will go limp and the flavour will be spoiled.

Cooked vegetables are served in a way that in Italian we call *condite*, which means with something added to improve the taste, usually olive oil and salt. Not many people add vinegar to them. Although in every country you can now get virtually anything, there are always things which will not be popular somewhere, and so you never see them. For instance, you never see runner beans in Italy. You never see curled parsley or garden mint for sale. You can only get wild mint, while the other type is grown purely for the confectionery industry. Corn on the cob is not eaten boiled and is never served as a vegetable at a dinner. It is only barbecued – roasted on charcoal – mainly at 'Ferragosto'. *Ferragosto* is the summer holiday which originates from the Roman festival *Feriae Augusti*. This festival used to be at the beginning of the month in honour of Augustus. Now it falls on 15 August and people take their annual holiday around this date. In August it is impossible to do anything or to find anybody. You better not be ill, either! Everybody seems to be somewhere else. All the factories and shops are also closed for about two or three weeks.

On the night of the 14th it was always the custom to make great bonfires in the countryside; you would see fires here and there, lighting up the dark night. On these hot summer's evenings it is great fun to cook the fresh cobs of corn in the open. You can, however, cook them just as well on an ordinary grill. The grains burst open and they become golden brown. When you buy corn, always make sure it is tender and fresh. Squeeze one grain between your thumb and one finger, and a milky juice should come out.

The custom of bonfires is dying out due to the danger of bush fires, and fireworks are getting more popular. The 15th is a day to be spent either on the beach, up a mountain or by a stream, as it is usually very hot, and it is customary to have a picnic. When Italians have picnics there is nothing skimpy or frugal about them. They manage to have an enormous meal, with all the courses that they would have at home on a special day. Nothing will be missing, from an *antipasto* to the hot pasta dish, probably *pasta al forno* or lasagne, and a mixture of roast meats, and it will end up with an oversized water melon. More water melons are consumed on this day than in the whole of the rest of the year, and everything will be washed down with generous helpings of local wine.

Picking corn to be used as animal fodder and for polenta has always been quite an affair in the villages. After the corn is cut, it is brought to the house, the leaves are removed and the corn is left outside in the sun for a few days to dry out completely. The leaves used to make up the filling of the poorer farmers' mattresses, while the better-off would have their mattresses filled with the fleeces from their sheep. When the corn is thoroughly dry, there is a gathering in one of the houses, when people help each other to pull the grains of corn from the cobs with a gadget called a *furicchio*. This will go on until the early hours, ending with *quattro salti* (four jumps), an improvised dance accompanied by the music of the village accordion virtuoso – the only incentive which draws the younger generation into participating in such a boring task!

Pomodori
Tomatoes

Tomatoes play a great part in Italian cooking, especially the pear-shaped ones (*pomodori a pera*) which you buy in tins. They are tastier for sauces than any other variety. When in season, they are used fresh, of course, and most of the families will preserve their own. Each housewife will have her very secret recipe which is passed from mother to daughter. This is mostly in the south of Italy, where these tomatoes are grown extensively for canning.

You can now buy strained tomatoes (*pomodori passati*). One 400g (15 oz) tin is equal to two 397g (14 oz) tins of peeled tomatoes. You can save a lot of time using strained tomatoes in sauces.

If you want to use fresh tomatoes for your sauces, you can use the round type, although the taste will be very different. But one thing you must not forget: they must be very ripe. Round tomatoes are best used for soups, for stuffing, grilling or eating raw in salads. You can grow pear-shaped tomatoes here, but to ripen properly they need a greenhouse, even when we get one of those rare glorious English summers! In Italy tomatoes used in salads are never ripe, but green or just slightly pink.

Insalata delle cappuccine
Cappucina Salad

I am sure everybody knows that a *cappuccino* is an espresso coffee with frothy milk and its name originates from the fact that its appearance reminds you of the habit of a *cappuccino* monk, a friar from the Order of St Francis of Assisi who wears a white hood. I am not so sure that many of you will know what a *cappuccina* is. Apart from being a nun from the religious order of the Cappuccine, it is also the name of a salad. It consists of a type of lettuce with small curly leaves and has special ingredients in the mixture. In my home town there is a convent where these Cappuccine nuns live. I think it is the only order whose affiliates are never allowed outside, not even for a death in their family. They only go outside to the walled garden of the convent from which they cannot see any other living soul. Their work involves cultivating their vegetables, making drinks from their own fruit, and embroidering garments to order, and they pray most of the hours of day and night. In the church, adjoining the convent, a bell tolls at hourly intervals, all night long, calling the nuns to prayer. That bell is a nightmare for people living nearby – and I used to be one of them. The nuns live off charity, and people can call at a door with a spy hole and leave their donations and presents on a turning wheel.

These nuns also make a delicious salad which I will describe. They do not sell it, but make it to give away as a thank you for gifts.

Cappuccina lettuce is a small-leaved variety, rather like the 'salad bowl' type, which you cut as it is needed and it goes on growing. When this lettuce is not in season, they use any salad ingredients available (including endive, chicory).

This salad is delicious, and a meal in itself.

Clean and wash enough salad for 4 persons. Drain it well, and chop finely. Then rub a garlic clove all around the salad bowl. Sprinkle salt, a little vinegar and some olive oil in the bowl, then mix it well. Now toast 8 slices of brown or white bread. Hardboil 4 eggs and cool them under the cold tap, then peel them. Sprinkle some olive oil mixed with the same amount of water on the toast, then place the slices all around the salad dish. Place the prepared salad on top of the bread, leaving a border of toast all the way round, then cut the eggs into quarters and place them in the middle of the green lettuce, in the shape of a yellow and white daisy.

Insalata di fagioli cannellini
Bean Salad

Fagioli cannellini are dry, thin and long beans. They take their name from the fact that they look like cinnamon sticks (*cannella*). You can make a similar salad using butter beans, for example.

Serves 4

250g (10 oz) fagioli cannellini beans
salt

freshly ground black pepper
olive oil

Wash the beans. Soak them overnight. Boil the beans until tender, then rinse in boiling water. Drain and set aside to cool. Season with salt and pepper, then coat with olive oil when cold.

Insalata mista
Mixed Salad

Rugola or *ruchetta* is a type of leaf tasting similar to endive
– a little bitter – which grows in the spring. In winter you
can use endive.

Serves 6

1 lettuce, shredded
1 bunch of radishes,
  chopped
6 garlic leaves, finely
  chopped

½ cucumber, chopped
about 12 leaves of rugola or
  ruchetta

For the dressing
salt
2 tablespoons vinegar or
  juice of ½ lemon

100ml (3½ fl oz) olive oil

Place all the salad ingredients in a large bowl and toss
gently until well mixed. Thoroughly mix together the
dressing ingredients and pour over the salad just before
serving.

Insalata di pomodori verdi
Green Tomato Salad

Serves 6

12 medium-sized green
   tomatoes, thinly sliced
100ml (3½ fl oz) olive oil
2 tablespoons vinegar or
   juice of ½ lemon

salt
freshly ground black
   pepper

Arrange the tomatoes on a serving platter. Mix together the remaining ingredients and pour over the tomatoes just before serving.

Insalata di pomodori e peperoni
Tomato and Pepper Salad

It is best to choose tomatoes which are just turning pink in colour.

Serves 4

5 medium-sized tomatoes,
   thinly sliced
2 large yellow or red
   peppers, cored, seeded
   and sliced

2 tablespoons olive oil
1½ tablespoons vinegar
salt

Arrange the tomato and pepper slices in a large salad bowl or serving platter. Mix together the remaining ingredients and pour over the tomatoes and peppers just before serving.

Insalata russa
Russian Salad

Serves 6

6 hardboiled eggs
4 medium-sized potatoes,
 boiled
450g (1 lb) packet frozen
 mixed vegetables
8 small artichokes

salt
homemade mayonnaise
 (page 61)
12 large black olives
6 anchovy fillets

Set aside the eggs and potatoes until completely cool. Prepare the mixed vegetables according to the packet instructions, drain and set aside to cool. Prepare the artichokes (see page 117) and set aside to cool. Finely dice the eggs, potatoes and artichokes and mix together with the vegetables. Place in a large salad bowl, add salt and spoon over the mayonnaise. Garnish with olives and anchovy fillets. Serve at once.

Insalata di mare
Seafood Salad

Serves 4–5

250g (10 oz) squid
1 small onion, *peeled and quartered*
1 celery stick, *chopped*
salt
175g (6 oz) *shelled prawns*
184g (6½ oz) *tin tuna*
juice of ½ lemon
2 tablespoons olive oil
4–5 leaves *fresh basil*
1 tablespoon *chopped fresh parsley*
1 small pimento, *chopped (optional) or freshly ground black pepper*

Clean the squid (see page 188). Place in a large saucepan with enough water to cover, adding the onion and celery. Season with salt. Simmer for about 1 hour until the squid are tender. In a separate pan boil the prawns for about 5 minutes, drain and leave to cool. Drain the squid, discarding the vegetables, and leave to cool. When cold, cut into strips and mix together with the prawns. Adjust the salt if necessary. Reserving the oil, drain and flake the tuna. Mix the tuna and its oil with the other fish, and add the lemon juice, olive oil, basil, parsley, pimento or black pepper. Mix well and serve at once.

Vegetables

Carciofi fritti
Fried Artichokes

Serves 4

5–6 artichokes
juice of 1 lemon
salt
flour for coating

1 egg, lightly beaten
oil for frying
4 lemon wedges for
   serving

Prepare the artichokes, by discarding the outside leaves, until you get to the very tender ones. Trim the ends, wash and cut the artichokes into very thin segments. Make about 10 slices out of every artichoke. Sprinkle the pieces with the lemon juice and salt. Roll the artichoke pieces in flour, then in the egg, coating them all over. Heat the oil

117

in a large frying pan and fry the artichokes, until they are all a golden-brown colour. Drain them on kitchen paper and keep hot until you finish frying. Serve with lemon wedges, adding pepper if you wish.

Carciofi alla parmigiana ⒡
Artichokes the Parmesan Way

Serves 4

5–6 artichokes	*25g (1 oz) margarine*
juice of 1 lemon	*2 tablespoons tomato*
salt	* purée*
flour for coating	*400ml (14 fl oz) water*
1 egg, lightly beaten	*3 tablespoons grated*
oil for frying	* Parmesan cheese*

Prepare the artichokes as in the previous recipe. Heat the oil in a large frying pan and fry the artichokes in batches. Set aside and keep hot. Melt the margarine in a large saucepan, adding salt and the tomato purée diluted in 3 tablespoons water. Stir while it comes to the boil, then add the remaining water, mix well and simmer for about 15 minutes.

Remove the pan from the heat. Pour 2 tablespoons of the cooking liquid into an ovenproof dish. Make a layer of the fried artichoke, and sprinkle some of the Parmesan cheese on top. Add some more of the cooking liquid, then continue making layers in the same way. When all the ingredients have been used, pour the remaining cooking liquid on top. Cover and bake in a preheated oven, at 140°C (325°F), gas mark 3, for about 30–40 minutes.

Carciofi 'alla giudia'
Artichokes the Roman Way

This typical Roman way of cooking artichokes is called *alla giudia*, a very obscure word, unless it stands for *giudea*, 'the Jewish way'.

If you buy artichokes in Italy, they will have the stalks, which are edible. Cut them off, peel them with a knife, cut them in pieces and add them to the saucepan with the remaining ingredients.

Serves 4

8 artichokes
juice of 1 lemon
25g (1 oz) parsley
½ clove garlic
salt

freshly ground black
   pepper
300ml (½ pint) water
100ml (3½ fl oz) olive oil

Discard a few outer leaves of the artichokes, but not too many, as you will be discarding the hard part of the outside leaves as you eat. With a very sharp knife, trim the ends of the leaves, with a slanting cut, so you cut more on the outside than on the inside leaves.

Wash the artichokes well and leave them for a few minutes in water in which you have squeezed the lemon juice. Chop the parsley and the garlic, and add salt and pepper. Remove the artichokes from the water, shake them dry, and open the leaves a little with your fingers. Sprinkle with salt, then push some of the parsley and garlic mixture in each one of the artichokes.

Use a saucepan large enough to hold all the artichokes standing up side by side, and arrange them next to each other. Pour the oil into the saucepan and a little of the water. Cover and simmer for at least 45 minutes. Check after the first 15 minutes and add the remaining water.

Spike one with a fork, right in the middle, to check if it is tender. They should be very soft when cooked.

Carciofi al tegame
Artichoke Casserole

Serves 4

artichokes	salt
juice of 1 lemon	freshly ground black
25g (1 oz) parsley	pepper
½ clove garlic	100ml (3½ fl oz) water
2 tablespoons olive oil	

Discard the outside leaves of the artichokes, until you get to the very tender ones. Trim and wash, then cut each artichoke into quarters, and each quarter into half. Sprinkle the pieces with lemon juice. Chop the parsley together with the garlic, and add both to a large saucepan with the oil. After a few moments over moderate heat, add the artichokes, season with salt and pepper, stir, then add the water. Cover and simmer, stirring from time to time, for about 30 minutes.

Carciofi bolliti alla parmigiana
Artichokes the Parmesan Way, with a Difference

Serves 4

6 artichokes	salt
juice of 1 lemon	freshly ground black
25g (1 oz) butter	`pepper
25g (1 oz) grated Parmesan	
cheese	

120

Prepare the artichokes as in the previous recipe, cutting each into 8 segments. Put them in a large saucepan over moderate heat, then cover with water. Squeeze in the lemon juice. Bring them to the boil and simmer for about 30 minutes. Drain the artichokes. Spread the butter over the bottom of an ovenproof dish, mix the artichokes with the Parmesan cheese, salt and pepper and place in the dish. Cover and bake in a preheated oven at 220°C (425°F), gas mark 7, for 10 minutes.

Torta di carciofi ⓕ
Artichoke Tart

This dish is delicious served as an accompaniment to meat, or as a course by itself.

Serves 6

6 artichokes
juice of 1 lemon
2 tablespoons olive oil
1 tablespoon chopped fresh
  parsley
50ml (2 fl oz) water
2 eggs, lightly beaten
225g (8 oz) ricotta

3 tablespoons grated
  Parmesan cheese
salt
freshly ground black
  pepper
225g (8 oz) self-raising
  flour
100g (4 oz) margarine

Cut the stalks off the artichokes and put them aside. Remove the outside leaves until you get to the tender ones (they will be lighter in colour). Trim the ends off. Wash and cut each into 8 segments. Sprinkle the lemon juice over the artichokes, so that they do not change colour. Heat the oil in a large saucepan over moderate heat and add the parsley, then the artichokes with the water. Cover and cook until tender, stirring occasionally. It will take about 25–30 minutes. Remove from the heat, drain any surplus cooking liquid and add the eggs, mixed with the ricotta, Parmesan cheese, salt and pepper. Mix all these ingredients together well and leave to cool.

Rub the flour and margarine together with the tips of your fingers until the mixture looks like fine breadcrumbs. Add a pinch of salt and mix with the water. Chill for 15 minutes, then roll out on a lightly floured surface. Grease a 23cm (9 inch) soufflé dish and line the bottom and sides with the pastry. Add the cold mixture into the dish and cover with the remaining pastry. Bake in a preheated oven at 190° (375°F), gas mark 5, for 30 minutes.

Asparagi
Asparagus

1 bundle asparagus
20g (¾ oz) grated Parmesan
   cheese
salt

freshly ground black
   pepper
50g (2 oz) butter

Clean the asparagus and cut off a little piece from the bottom of each stem. Wash and tie them in a bundle. If you don't have an asparagus cooker, take the tallest saucepan you have with a lid and place the asparagus in it, heads up. The bundle should cook standing up. Do not cover with water, but add enough water to cover them halfway up the stems. Bring to the boil and simmer until tender. When they are ready, the tips will bend down. Drain and place them in a serving dish. Sprinkle the grated Parmesan cheese over the top, and season with salt and pepper. Melt the

butter and when very hot, pour it over the asparagus.
Cover the asparagus and leave for 5 minutes in a hot place
before serving.

Melanzane alla parmigiana Ⓕ
Aubergines the Parmesan Way

Serves 4

*1.5kg (3 lb) aubergines
salt
flour for coating
1 egg, lightly beaten
oil for frying
450ml (¾ pint) water*

*2 tablespoons tomato
  purée
25g (1 oz) margarine
30g (1¼ oz) grated
  Parmesan cheese*

Scrape and wash the aubergines, then cut them in half and
slice lengthwise. Season with salt, roll them in flour, then
in the beaten egg. Fry the aubergine slices in hot oil turning
until golden, then drain on a piece of kitchen paper. In a
saucepan over moderate heat, boil the water, mix in the
tomato purée and the margarine, and season. Boil for 15
minutes. Pour a little of this liquid in an ovenproof dish,
make a layer of the fried aubergines, sprinkle with grated
Parmesan, then make another layer of aubergines and
continue until all the ingredients are used. Pour the rest of
the cooking liquid on top. Bake in a preheated oven at
220°C (425°F), gas mark 7, for 15 minutes.

Melanzane al tegame
Aubergine Casserole

Serves 4

1.5kg (3 lb) aubergines
100ml (3½ fl oz) olive oil
1 medium-sized onion,
  peeled and chopped

2 tablespoons chopped fresh
  parsley
½ clove garlic
200ml (7½ fl oz) water

Scrape the aubergines and cut them into cubes. Heat the olive oil in a deep frying pan and fry the onion until tender. Add the parsley, garlic (in one piece, so you can remove it at the end of cooking) and the aubergines. Cook, stirring often, adding the water after about 15 minutes. Continue cooking for another 20 minutes or until the aubergines are soft.

Fagiolini al pomodoro
Green Beans with Tomatoes

I find this way of cooking green beans is a good change when you get fed up with green beans served in butter or oil.

Serves 4

400g (14 oz) beans
1 medium-sized onion,
  peeled and chopped
2 tablespoons corn oil

5 ripe tomatoes, skinned,
  seeded and chopped
freshly ground black
  pepper

Top and tail the beans, if you're using French beans, or clean and slice them. Boil them in salted water until tender, and drain. In a large frying pan over a moderate heat, cook the onion in the oil for 3–5 minutes until tender. Add the tomatoes, stir and cook for 10 minutes, then add the beans and season. Stir occasionally and cook for a further 15 minutes.

Cardoni o cardi
Cardoons

Cardoons look very much like a big celery, and the plant resembles the artichoke plant. You eat the thick stems when they are still tender, before they have produced a flower. The stems are tied up to whiten them. Cooked in certain ways, they taste like artichokes. In slang they are called *i gobbi* (a *gobbo* is a hunchback). I can only think that, tied up in a bundle, then bent down to be covered with earth for blanching, they must have given somebody the idea of hunchbacks at the bottom of the garden: a change from the usual fairies or gnomes of British origin!

Cardoni gratinati
Cardoons au Gratin

Serves 6

1 cardoon
salt
juice of ½ lemon
50g (2 oz) flour
300ml (½ pint) milk
1 teaspoon margarine

50g (2 oz) butter
25g (1 oz) grated Parmesan
   cheese
freshly ground black
   pepper

Scrape the stems or ribs of the cardoon, peeling off the outside and cutting away any prickles. Wash and cut them in sections, about 7.5cm (3 inches) long. Place them in a large saucepan with water and bring them to the boil, adding salt and the lemon juice. Boil for 10 minutes, then drain. Prepare a sauce by mixing the flour with a little of the milk. When smooth, add the remaining milk, the margarine and salt, then stir continuously over moderate heat until it thickens. Remove from the heat. Put the cardoon in an ovenproof dish with knobs of butter here and there, pour the sauce on the top and sprinkle with grated Parmesan cheese. Season with pepper. Bake in a preheated oven at 215°C (420°F), gas mark 7, for 10 minutes until brown.

Finocchi gratinati
Fennels au Gratin

You can cook fennel in the same way as the cardoons. You prepare the fennels by cutting them at the base to remove the rest of the stem, then divide them into quarters or into 6 segments. Wash these, then drop them in salted boiling water to cook for 10 minutes. Proceed as in the previous recipe.

Cardoni fritti
Fried Cardoons

Serves 5–6

1 cardoon
salt
juice of 1 lemon
flour for coating

1 egg, lightly beaten
oil for frying
lemon wedges for serving

Scrape the cardoon stems, peeling the outside skin, and removing the prickles. Wash them, cut into segments, then boil in a large saucepan of salted water with the lemon juice. Boil for 10 minutes, drain and roll the pieces in flour, then in the beaten egg. Heat the oil in a large fan, then fry the cardoon and drain on kitchen paper. Serve with lemon wedges.

Cardoni alla parmigiana ⒻSmart
Cardoons the Parmesan Way

Serves 6

1 cardoon
salt
juice of 1 lemon
flour for coating
1 egg, lightly beaten
oil for frying
2 tablespoons tomato
   purée

25g (1 oz) margarine
freshly ground black
   pepper
450ml (¾ pint) water
35g (1½ oz) grated
   Parmesan cheese

Prepare and fry the cardoon as in the previous recipe. In a large saucepan, dilute the tomato purée in 200ml (7½ fl oz) water, add the margarine, and season. Bring to the boil, then add the water and bring to the boil again. Simmer for 15 minutes, then remove from the heat. Pour 3–4 tablespoons of the cooking liquid into a large ovenproof dish, then add a layer of the fried cardoon and sprinkle about 2 tablespoons Parmesan on top, then some of the liquid. Continue with these layers until you have used up all the ingredients. Cover and bake in a preheated oven at 220°C (425°F), gas mark 7, for 15 minutes.

Cavolfiori in salsa piccante
Cauliflower in Piquant Sauce

Serves 4

1 medium-sized cauliflower

For the sauce
juice of ½ lemon
1 preserved pepper
1 gherkin

4–5 anchovy fillets
3 tablespoons olive oil

Prepare the sauce before cooking the cauliflower. Squeeze the lemon juice on to the pepper. (This isn't necessary if the pepper is preserved in vinegar.) Chop the pepper, with the gherkin and the anchovies, and mash together into a pulp. (You can use a liquidizer if you wish.) Mix this pulp with the olive oil. Break the cauliflower into florets and cook until tender. Drain into a serving dish and pour the sauce on top, mixing gently.

Zucchine ripiene
Stuffed Baby Marrows or Courgettes

Serves 4

4 baby marrows or
 courgettes
salt
20g (¾ oz) parsley
⅓ clove garlic

40g (1½ oz) breadcrumbs
2 tablespoons olive oil
freshly ground black
 pepper
margarine for greasing

Choose fairly large courgettes: they must be at least 4cm (1½ inches) in diameter. Using an apple corer if you have one, scoop out the centre of each courgette and discard. Sprinkle the insides with salt. To prepare the filling, chop the parsley with the garlic, then add the breadcrumbs and olive oil and season. Place the courgettes in a large saucepan over a moderate heat, cover with water and bring to the boil. Add a little salt to the water and simmer for 5 minutes. Drain them, reserving the cooking liquid, then stuff with the filling, being careful not to break them while you push the filling inside with the end of a small spoon. Grease an ovenproof dish with a little margarine, add the courgettes with a small knob of margarine. Cover and bake in a preheated oven at 200°C (400°F), gas mark 6, for 1 hour and pour over the cooking liquid. When ready, cut the courgettes in half lengthwise on a serving dish. As an alternative, you can make a tomato sauce, as for the stuffed peppers on page 139.

Zucchine in padella
Baby Marrows in the Frying Pan

Serves 4

450g (1 lb) baby marrows
100ml (3½ fl oz) olive oil
1 large onion, peeled and
  thinly sliced
250g (10 oz) very ripe
  tomatoes, skinned,
  seeded and chopped

salt
freshly ground black
  pepper

Top and tail, wash and cut the courgettes in half. If they are very small and fresh, cut them in pieces as they are, otherwise discard the middle, where the seeds are. Heat the oil in a large frying pan over moderate heat and fry the onion for 3–5 minutes until tender. Add the tomatoes and courgettes and season with salt and pepper. Cover and simmer for about 45 minutes, stirring often. If it gets too dry, add 100ml (3½ fl oz) water. Stir often. Keep covered.

Funghi ripieni
Stuffed Mushrooms

Serves 4

10 large mushrooms
4 tablespoons olive oil
1 tablespoon chopped fresh
* parsley*
½ clove garlic, chopped
1 medium-sized onion,
* peeled and chopped*

3 anchovy fillets, chopped
freshly ground black
* pepper*
2 tablespoons fresh white
* breadcrumbs*

Choose large mushrooms. Wash the two smallest mushrooms, take off the stalks with a sharp knife, and cut them into very small pieces. Place 2 tablespoons of the oil in a large saucepan and fry the parsley, garlic, onion and anchovy fillets for 5 minutes, adding a little pepper. Remove from the heat and mix in the breadcrumbs.

Now prepare the remaining mushrooms. Scrape and wash them well, sprinkle with a little salt, then fill each with some of the mixture, pressing down with your fingers. Sprinkle a few more breadcrumbs on top, with a few drops of olive oil on top of each mushroom. Place them in a greased ovenproof dish. Bake in a preheated oven at 215°C (420°F), gas mark 7, for 20 minutes.

Funghi in padella
Mushrooms in the Pan

In my opinion, this is the best and quickest way of cooking mushrooms.

Serves 4

150g (6 oz) mushrooms
2 tablespoons olive oil
2 tablespoons fresh chopped
   parsley

½ clove garlic
freshly ground black
   pepper
salt

Scrape the mushrooms, peel the stalks, wash them and cut into quarters or slices. Heat the olive oil in a large frying pan, with the parsley, garlic (in one piece), pepper and salt. Cook quickly stirring often, for 10–15 minutes. Discard the garlic and serve.

Piselli al grasso e magro
Peas with Unsmoked Streaky Bacon

Fresh peas are best, but you can use frozen ones.

Serves 4

25g (1 oz) margarine
1 medium-sized onion,
   peeled and chopped
4 slices unsmoked streaky
   rindless bacon, chopped
6 fresh chopped basil leaves
   or a pinch dry basil

300g (12 oz) shelled peas
salt
freshly ground black
   pepper
1 beef stock cube
175ml (6 fl oz) water

Melt the margarine in a large saucepan over moderate heat and fry the onion for about 5 minutes, until soft. Add the bacon and basil. Cook very slowly so that all the fat melts and the bacon is crisp. Add the peas and season. Dissolve the stock cube in the water, and stir in. Boil for 15 minutes, stirring from time to time. Drain and serve hot.

Piselli al prosciutto
Peas with Parma Ham

Serves 4

1 beef stock cube
225ml (8 fl oz) boiling
   water
50g (2 oz) butter
1 medium-sized onion,
   peeled and chopped

300g (12 oz) shelled peas
3 slices prosciutto,
   chopped

Dissolve the beef cube in the boiling water. Melt the butter in a large saucepan and fry the onion in the butter until soft. Add the stock and the peas and boil quickly for 15 minutes. Remove the pan from the heat and add the ham, mixing everything thoroughly. Drain and serve hot.

Patate lessate
Boiled Potatoes

It seems ridiculous to tell anybody how to boil potatoes, but I always find it very strange that people seem to peel their potatoes before they boil them, while in Italy nobody does so. Why go to all the trouble of scraping and peeling, making a mess of your hands, when you need only wash, boil and then peel them very easily? There is also the advantage that if sometimes you cook them a little too long, they do not get full of water. After the potatoes are peeled, add salt and pepper, a sprinkle of olive oil and mix in a little chopped fresh parsley. Shake the pan and serve at once.

Patate alla svizzera
Potatoes the Swiss Way

In northern Italy, you will find that some of the cooking is influenced by the eating habits of the country across the border.

Serves 6

1kg (2 lb) potatoes
salt
freshly ground black
* pepper*
100g (4 oz) margarine

100g (4 oz) fresh pecorino
* or Cheddar cheese,*
* grated*
4 tablespoons grated
* Parmesan cheese*

Wash the potatoes and boil them in their skin. They will need about 30–40 minutes. Prod them with a fork to make sure they are tender. When cooked, peel and slice. Season with salt and pepper. Take an ovenproof dish, grease with a little of the margarine, then layer alternately with the potatoes and *pecorino* or cheddar cheese. Repeat the layers until you have used up all the ingredients, placing small knobs of margarine between the layers, here and there. Cover with the grated Parmesan. Bake in a preheated oven at 215°C (420°F), gas mark 7, for 20 minutes.

Patate con cipolle
Potatoes with Onions

Serves 4

1kg (2 lb) potatoes
salt
freshly ground black
  pepper
40g (1½ oz) margarine

4 large onions
175ml (6 fl oz) milk
2 teaspoons butter

Wash the potatoes and boil them in their skin. When cooked, drain and peel them. Cut them into slices and season. Melt the margarine in a large frying pan and cook the onion until tender, stirring often. Grease a large ovenproof dish, then layer alternately the potatoes and onions, repeating until you have used them all. Pour the milk on top and add small knobs of butter. Cover and bake for 30 minutes in a preheated oven at 200°C (400°F), gas mark 6–7.

Spinaci gratinati
Spinach au Gratin

Serves 4

500g (17 oz) spinach
salt
freshly ground black
  pepper

25g (1 oz) butter
25g (1 oz) grated Parmesan
  cheese

Wash the spinach. Drain and cook in a large saucepan without adding any water, stirring often until the spinach is tender. Add salt and pepper. Tip the spinach into an ovenproof dish, add the butter and sprinkle with the Parmesan. Cook in a preheated oven at 200°C (400°F), gas mark 7, for 10 minutes.

Spinaci in padella
Spinach in the Frying Pan

Serves 4

500g (17 oz) spinach
2 whole anchovies or 4
  anchovy fillets
25g (1 oz) butter

freshly ground black
  pepper
salt

Wash the spinach and drain well. Put the spinach in a large frying pan and cook without adding any water, stirring often until the spinach is tender. Clean the anchovies (if you are using the salty ones) and chop finely. If there is water left in the pan after the spinach is tender, drain it, then mix in the butter, the anchovies and pepper, but only a little salt. Stir well.

Pomodori ripieni
Stuffed Tomatoes

Serves 4

4 large nearly ripe tomatoes, pink-red in colour

salt

2 tablespoons chopped fresh parsley

½ clove garlic, chopped

40g (1¾ oz) fresh white breadcrumbs

freshly ground black pepper

3 tablespoons olive oil

Wash the tomatoes and cut them in half horizontally. Remove the seeds. Sprinkle with a little salt and turn upside down to drain. Mix the parsley and garlic with the breadcrumbs, season and add 2 tablespoons of oil, mixing everything well together. Fill the cavity of each tomato half with this mixture. Place all the filled tomatoes on a greased baking sheet or an ovenproof dish and put a few drops of olive oil on each half. Bake in a preheated oven at 215°C (420°F), gas mark 7, for 25 minutes. The breadcrumbs on top should be golden brown.

Peperoni
Peppers

The peppers for the following recipes can be green, yellow or red. I usually mix them, but it is up to you which ones you prefer to cook, as the yellow and red ones are sweeter than the green. Some Italians now skin their peppers because, they say, the skin can give you indigestion, but in my home we eat peppers, skin and all. If you do want to skin the peppers, hold them with a fork on top of a gas flame or under a grill until the skin detaches itself from the flesh, bursting in places. Then dip the peppers in cold water and scrape the skin off with your fingers and the help of a sharp knife. Most of the skin will come away, but you cannot be too fussy. Personally, to go through this operation puts me off cooking peppers altogether, so I only do it for Italian guests!

All Italians follow the fashion. Italians are very fashion-conscious people: not only do they feel the need to renovate their clothes every season, but their body will acquire symptoms of different illnesses in different years. One year it is fashionable to eat something, next year the same thing will be deadly poisonous to your system for one reason or another. One summer, everybody will get liver trouble, appendicitis the next, while having your blood pressure checked is an imperative weekly pastime. I am often asked what my blood pressure is and my friends are astonished that I do not bother to find out. So, now you should not eat peppers with their skin!

Peperoni ripieni
Stuffed Peppers

Serves 4

4 large peppers, green,
  yellow or red
salt
2 tablespoons chopped fresh
  parsley
½ clove garlic, chopped
40g (1¾ oz) fresh white
  breadcrumbs
100g (4 oz) cooked minced
  meat

freshly ground black
  pepper
1 egg, lightly beaten
1 tablespoon olive oil
1 tablespoon tomato purée
1 teaspoon margarine
300ml (½ pint) water
1 tablespoon cornflour
1 tablespoon water
a pinch of nutmeg

Wash the peppers, remove a thin slice from the base, cut off the tops and remove the cores and seeds from the centres. Sprinkle a little salt inside the peppers and leave them aside. To prepare the stuffing, mix together the parsley, garlic, breadcrumbs and minced meat. Season and bind this mixture with the beaten egg. Stuff the peppers then place them upright in a greased ovenproof dish and sprinkle just a few drops of olive oil on top. Cover and cook them in a preheated oven at 200°C (400°F), gas mark 6, for about 1 hour. Make sure they are tender and cooked through by prodding them with a fork. Cut them in half lengthwise with a sharp knife. Arrange them on a serving dish and keep hot.

To prepare the sauce, mix the tomato purée with the margarine, salt and water. Boil for 15 minutes. Mix the cornflour with 1 tablespoon water and add it to the sauce, stirring it in well. Boil for 1 minute more, then pour over the peppers and sprinkle with nutmeg.

Peperonata [Ⓕ]
Casseroled Peppers

Serves 4

6 *large peppers*
100ml *(3½ fl oz) olive or*
  corn oil
1 *medium-sized onion,*
  peeled and chopped
6 *very ripe tomatoes,*
  skinned, seeded and
  chopped

salt
freshly ground black
  pepper

Wash the peppers and cut them in half, remove the seeds, then cut them into smaller pieces. Heat the oil in a large saucepan over moderate heat and cook the onion for about 3 minutes until soft, stirring it often. Add the peppers and the tomatoes to the onion, season with salt and pepper and simmer for about 30 minutes, or until the peppers are soft. Stir occasionally. If the peppers are not soft after 30 minutes, add ½ tumbler of water, bring it to the boil, and simmer for a further 15–20 minutes.

Frittura mista di verdura
Fried Mixed Vegetables

Frying different vegetables together makes a very tasty and interesting mixture, but obviously you can also use just one type at a time. Cauliflower, globe or Jerusalem artichokes, cardoons, celery, aubergines, courgettes and marrow flowers are all suitable for frying. Vegetables such as cauliflower, cardoons, celery and Jerusalem artichokes need more preparation than the rest because, apart from cleaning, scraping and chopping, they must be boiled first, then drained, and rolled in flour and beaten egg before being fried.

Aubergines, courgettes and marrow flowers should be washed, cut in pieces, then sprinkled with salt and left to drain for 15 minutes before being coated with flour and beaten egg and fried. These vegetables must be cut very thinly; the courgettes in thin circles, the aubergines in thin slices, after removing the seeds. The flowers are just cut in sections.

4

Pasta, Polenta and Pizza

Pasta

In this chapter you will find ways of preparing pasta dishes like lasagne and cappelletti that are for special occasions. But before I embark on the recipes, I must emphasize that homemade pasta is essential for these specialities. You must be prepared to make your own – or to buy fresh pasta, if you are lucky enough to live near a shop that sells it (see page 281). In this age of gadgets, making pasta is a very simplified task. There are many machines on the market which are all very easy to operate, and once you start to make your own you will certainly not go back to packets. The machines are not expensive and they last a lifetime.

Strange as it may seem, in Italy some people still make

their own pasta by hand. I was recently visiting a friend in Rome and saw, to my astonishment, that her maid was making fresh pasta by hand. In days gone by, peasant girls getting ready for marriage were supposed to be expert in ironing and folding men's shirts, and making pasta. They would be considered experts when they could roll out the dough into a perfect circle. To roll out pasta by hand you need a very long rolling pin, because to stretch the amount of dough you get by using, say, two eggs, you will end up with a circle approximately two and a half feet in diameter, so your rolling pin must be at least three feet long.

When I got married and came to England, I could not get a rolling pin the right size, so a kind uncle of my husband made me one, after long and detailed explanations about its thickness and length. I think he only offered to make the thing because he was fascinated by the idea of seeing what I was going to do with it. Fortunately for me, he had no notion of what to expect. I was no expert rolling-pin user and the shapes of my end product turned out as a mixture of oblongs with no resemblance whatsoever to Giotto's 'O'. The result, however, once cooked, was a complete success and since then many guests have praised my efforts.

You may be wondering what Giotto's 'O' is. The story goes that Pope Benedict IX wanted some paintings done and sent a courtier to find out who were the best painters of the time. He stopped at many artists' workshops and took from each one of them a sample of his work. When he arrived at Giotto's place and asked for one of his drawings, Giotto took a sheet of paper, dipped a brush in colour and without moving his arm drew a perfect circle, just with a twist of his hand. This he gave as a sample of his work to the astonished Pope's messenger. When the Pope looked at all the drawings, he asked the courtier to describe how Giotto had painted that circle. When he heard, the only painter he wanted at his court was Giotto. Since then, Giotto's 'O' has become the synonym for perfection.

How to Make Fresh Pasta

Serves 2–3

2 eggs   *225g (8 oz) plain flour*

Fix the machine on your kitchen table. Put half of the flour into a large mixing bowl. Crack the eggs one by one. When you use a number of eggs, it is always advisable to crack one egg at a time in a separate basin, in case there is a bad one. Tip the cracked eggs in the middle of the flour, beat them lightly with a fork and gradually mix with the flour, adding more until you have a stiff dough. Turn on to a lightly floured board, knead and roll it with your hands. Knead it roughly, then cut off one piece. If you have used 2 eggs to make pasta, then cut dough into 4 pieces. Use one at a time and keep the rest in the mixing bowl, covered with a damp cloth, so it will not dry up and form a crust on top.

Using some flour, roll the first piece in the machine with the rollers as far apart as possible, adding flour when needed. Roll and fold the pasta again a few more times, putting it through the rollers at the same opening. When the dough is smooth and elastic and not at all sticky, change the width of the rollers to the last notch and put the pasta through. If the strip tears, it means it is too thin, so adjust the rollers to the next notch before repeating the operation. The strip of pasta will be thin and long. Being careful not to let it stick while you handle it, place it on the table on a clean cloth dusted with flour. Use up all the pieces of dough in the same way.

When you make pasta, remember to use plain flour and do not, on any account, be tempted to add water to the eggs. This would spoil your pasta, making it brittle during cooking and less tasty. In Italy you would be regarded as a mean person, and friends would avoid being guests in a household where the cook puts water in the pasta!

Some people add salt to the dough when mixing pasta, but I prefer to put it into the boiling water I cook it in, just as the water comes to the boil. You may also add a tablespoon of olive oil to the water which helps to prevent the pieces of pasta sticking to one another, but if you follow the main rules, you won't find this necessary.

To cook pasta you need a large deep saucepan, plenty of water and plenty of room for stirring. When the water boils, add the salt and drop the pasta in while you stir. Drop it in quickly, because if you hold it on top of the pan too long the steam will make it stick even before it gets into the water. Boil fresh homemade pasta for about 2 minutes, stirring from time to time. When you are ready to drain it, remove the pan from the heat and pour in a cup of cold water to stop it continuing to cook. Overcooked pasta is something Italians abhor.

Pasta verde
Green Pasta

Serves 2–3

50g (2 oz) spinach   *2 eggs*

See recipe for making tagliatelle, page 164. *Pasta verde* is made by adding some cooked, drained and very finely chopped spinach to the beaten eggs when you mix the dough.

Ragù Ⓕ

Ragù is a basic sauce which you can use with all types of pasta. It is best to buy tomato purée in small tins because if you do not use it all it will go dark in colour and dry up. When you open a tin, put the leftover purée in a glass container or a plastic tub, cover with cling film and keep it in the refrigerator. I do not buy purée in tubes because a lot of it gets wasted and also trying to squeeze out the right amount in a hurry drives me mad!

If you do not possess a mincer, you can use minced meat – the sauce will be thicker from the start – but see that there is not too much fat or gristle.

You can freeze this sauce. If you are making a double quantity or more for this purpose, divide the amount accordingly when partly frozen. Put the sauce in a freezer-proof container, leave it for a couple of hours in the coldest part of your freezer. It will be ready to cut when it is firm to the touch. Tip the sauce on a board and cut it into squares. Wrap each piece in foil and return it to the freezer. It will keep for months and you will be able to improvise a good dish of pasta at very short notice. If you have enough *ragù* for, say, 4 persons, and you get an unexpected guest, do not panic. There is a way of stretching your sauce. When your pasta is cooked, put it in a large dish still dripping a little, then mix a knob of butter with it, before pouring on the *ragù*.

One final word of advice: do not forget to cut the sauce before it is completely frozen. If you leave it in the freezer for a long time you will need a hammer and chisel to be able to use it – which once happened to me!

Serves 6

50g (2 oz) margarine
1 small onion, peeled and
  finely chopped
1 medium-sized carrot,
  chopped
1 stick celery, chopped, or
  2 celery leaves
4 fresh basil leaves,
  chopped, or a pinch of dry
  basil
salt

freshly ground black
  pepper
225g (8 oz) stewing steak or
  mince
2 397g (14 oz) tins peeled
  tomatoes
2 tablespoons tomato
  purée
250ml (8 fl oz) water

Melt the margarine in a large saucepan and fry the onion for 3–5 minutes until soft. Add the carrot, celery, basil, salt and pepper. Cook for about 1 minute, stirring. Add the meat and cook for a further 15 minutes, stirring occasionally. Strain the tomato juice into the saucepan through a fine sieve, using the back of a wooden spoon to extract all the pulp. There shouldn't be any seeds in the sauce. Dilute the tomato purée with the water and add to the saucepan.

Let the sauce come to the boil, then reduce the heat and cook gently for about 1½ hours, adding some water during the cooking process and stirring from time to time. At this stage the sauce should not be too thick.

When the meat is tender, remove the sauce from the heat, use a slotted spoon to lift out the meat and the vegetables and mince together. (I throw the celery away as I like only the flavour and it can become a bit stringy.) Return the minced meat to the pan, stir in the liquid sauce and your *ragù* is ready.

Pasta in bianco (al burro)
Plain Pasta (with Butter)

Serves 1 (main course)

100g (4 oz) pasta per person

25g (1 oz) butter or margarine

20g (¾ oz) grated Parmesan cheese

The easiest and quickest way of preparing any type of pasta is to serve it *in bianco*, literally 'in white'. This means without a sauce of any kind. Just mix the boiled, drained pasta with the butter or margarine and sprinkle the grated cheese on top. When you want to eat pasta this way it is wise not to drain it too well or it will be a little doughy. In some parts of Italy they just mix it with a little olive oil, but this is a dish mainly reserved for invalids. The Italians reckon that if you are not well you should eat *in bianco*. Italy is full of hypochondriacs who avoid eating pasta or any other dish with a sauce. '*Senza sugo per me*', 'without sauce for me' (*sugo* is sauce, but literally means juice), is the call of anybody who fears for the wellbeing of their liver, kidney, stomach or whatever.

As I've said before, in Italy everything goes in trends. At one time you were not supposed to use too much olive oil: 'It is too heavy; you should mix it with a little corn oil or sunflower oil' (which the year before was frowned upon). Another time you were supposed to try not to eat any butter, even with your pasta *in bianco*, so a friend of mine solved the problem by using a good deal of tomato juice (boiled for half an hour) on her pasta, and then covering the top with double cream! What amazes me is that so many people think they know all about ailments, tests, operations, medicines and remedies. Either they must know the equivalent of *Pears Encyclopaedia* by heart, or the doctors must be far more loquacious than their British counterparts, because I have not come across this phenomenon here. So, when in Italy, I must not poke scorn at them. I just listen to the real and imaginary illnesses and try to be very understanding.

There are some tasty variations to pasta *in bianco*, such as adding some very small pieces of ham, frankfurters or boiled courgettes, for example.

Salsa di magro Ⓕ
Meatless Sauce

Magro literally means 'lean', but in this instance it means 'without any meat or animal fat'. This sauce used to be the favourite on Fridays when they were considered meatless days in Catholic countries. It's just as good with spaghetti as with other homemade pasta.

Serves 5–6

50g (1¾ oz) tin filleted anchovies or 75g (3 oz) salted ones (page 58)
170g (6 oz) tin tuna (Italian or Portuguese)
4 tablespoons fresh parsley

½ clove garlic
50ml (2 fl oz) olive oil
2 397g (14 oz) tins peeled tomatoes
125ml (4 fl oz) water

Drain the anchovies and tuna, reserving the oil. Mix together the anchovies and the tuna, add the parsley and garlic and chop until a sort of paste is formed. Put the olive oil in a saucepan over a moderate heat, add the paste and the reserved fish oil. Fry for about 5 minutes, stirring from time to time, then add the strained tomatoes with the water. Simmer for about 45 minutes. Do not put salt in this sauce as the anchovies and tuna are already quite salty. You are not supposed to use any cheese with this sauce, but it is a matter of taste.

Salsa al pesto [Ⓕ]
Pesto Sauce

'Pesto' sauce gets its name from the verb *pestare* (to pound with a pestle), because in the years before liquidizers the ingredients used to be pounded in a mortar.

Serves 4

50g (2 oz) fresh basil	85ml (3 fl oz) olive oil
50g (2 oz) fresh parsley	salt
1 clove garlic	
50g (2 oz) grated Parmesan cheese	

Wash the basil and parsley and squeeze out the water. These herbs must be chopped very finely as the end product must look like a paste, so the best way is to use a liquidizer. Add the garlic to the liquidizer. Blend for a few moments until finely minced, transfer to a large basin, add the grated Parmesan and, stirring with a wooden spoon, gradually add the olive oil. It should not have any lumps. Season with salt. When you have cooked your pasta, add 2 tablespoons of the boiling water to the pesto, mix well then pour it on the strained pasta. Mix thoroughly.

Salsa alle vongole [Ⓕ]
Cockle Sauce

Serves 4

1kg (2 lb) cockles
a sprig of parsley, chopped
100ml (3½ fl oz) olive oil
½ clove garlic
4 tablespoons tomato
  purée

200ml (7 fl oz) water
salt
freshly ground black
  pepper

Wash the cockles in a bowl full of water to get rid of the sand. Scrape and rinse them several times. Put them in a large saucepan, cover and heat gently, shaking the pan. After a few moments the cockles will start to open. Remove them with a slotted spoon as they open. Discard any that do not open. Remove from their shells and set aside, reserving the cooking liquid. Place the parsley in a large saucepan over moderate heat with the olive oil and garlic, and cook for a few minutes. Add the cooking liquid and stir. Add the tomato purée diluted in the water, and season. Simmer for about 30 minutes, then add the cockles and boil for a further 5 minutes. Discard the garlic.

Serve with any type of pasta, but I'd particularly recommend it with spaghetti or fettuccine (very thinly cut tagliatelle). You are not supposed to add any cheese to pasta served with a fish sauce.

Salsa alle noci
Walnut Sauce

This sauce is traditionally eaten with spaghetti on

Christmas Eve. In my grandmother's day we had it every year, without exception.

Serves 2

50g (2 oz) walnuts
25g (1 oz) fresh parsley
50ml (2 fl oz) olive oil
salt

freshly ground black
 pepper
grated Parmesan cheese
 (optional)

Roughly chop the walnuts and parsley. Fry these ingredients in the olive oil for 10 minutes, adding salt and pepper. Sprinkle Parmesan cheese on top if you like.

Salsa porchetta
Porchetta Sauce

This sauce takes its name from a particular way of cooking a whole piglet *in porchetta*, stuffed with spices and herbs, mainly fennel.

Serves 2

50ml (2 fl oz) olive oil
about 150g (5 oz) pork
 fillet, cubed
25g (1 oz) chopped fresh
 wild fennel or 1 teaspoon
 fennel seeds
½ clove garlic, crushed
a small piece of pimento

a sprig of rosemary
65ml (2½ fl oz) white
 wine
homemade pasta (see page
 144)
3 tablespoons grated
 Parmesan cheese

Heat the oil in a large saucepan over moderate heat and fry the meat, fennel, garlic, pimento and rosemary for 5–6 minutes, then add the wine and cook for 30 more minutes, at low heat. Cook the pasta and mix the sauce with it, adding the grated Parmesan on top.

Salsa con piselli freschi
Fresh Pea Sauce

You can make this sauce with frozen peas when fresh ones are not available, but the taste of the two is quite different. You can also use small pieces of fried courgettes and cream, or aubergines and cream, with grated Parmesan added.

Serves 4–5

4 slices unsmoked streaky bacon, diced
1 medium-sized onion, peeled and chopped
450g (1 lb) fresh peas, shelled
4 chopped fresh basil leaves
3 tablespoons tomato purée

300ml (½ pint) water
salt
freshly ground black pepper
homemade pasta (see page 144)
50g (2 oz) grated Parmesan cheese

Place the bacon and onion in a saucepan and cook them very slowly until the onion is soft. Add the peas and basil and stir from time to time. After about 4 minutes, dilute the tomato purée in 100ml (3½ fl oz) of the water, add to the peas and season. Gradually add the remaining water. Simmer for 30 minutes. Serve with hot pasta and sprinkle with Parmesan cheese.

Salsa carbonara
Charcoal Maker's Sauce

Pecorino romano is supposed to be used for this sauce and it is very strong. If you like milder cheese, I suggest you use *sardo* (Sardinian), but buy the best type. There is a cheap type on the market which is like blotting paper.

Serves 2

25g (1 oz) margarine
1 medium-sized onion, peeled and chopped
4 slices unsmoked, streaky, rindless bacon, diced

homemade pasta (page 144)
1 egg, lightly beaten
40g (1½ oz) grated pecorino cheese

Melt the margarine in a large frying pan and cook the onion and bacon until the onion is soft and the bacon crisp. Meanwhile, boil the pasta, drain and place in a warmed serving dish. Quickly mix the egg with the pasta, then add the hot bacon and onion and mix. Spread *pecorino* cheese on top.

Salsa con salsicce e grasso e magro
Italian Sausage and Unsmoked Bacon Sauce

Grasso e magro is fresh streaky bacon.

Serves 4

6 slices unsmoked streaky
  bacon, diced
1 medium-sized onion,
  peeled and chopped
2 397g (14 oz) tins peeled
  tomatoes

4 Italian sausages
homemade pasta (page
  144)
50g (2 oz) grated Parmesan
  cheese

Place the bacon and onion in a large frying pan over
moderate heat and fry very slowly, stirring very often or it
will stick. When the onion is soft, add the strained
tomatoes. Simmer for 20 minutes, then add the sausages to
the sauce. Simmer for a further 15 minutes, adding 2
tablespoons of water. Make sure the sausages are cooked
before serving over pasta, sprinkled with Parmesan cheese.
There is no need to add salt, because the sausages and
bacon are already salted.

Cannelloni Ⓕ

Cannelloni are very large lasagne. They are arranged in a
dish in one layer only and they have a very thin cover of
white sauce on top. You can make them using the same
recipe as for lasagne (page 162). Just cut the squares of
pasta about double the size, then put in double the amount
of meat and arrange them in a dish with Parmesan and a
good amount of *ragù* (meat and tomato sauce) on top.
Cover them with the white sauce and bake them in a
preheated oven at 220°C (425°F), gas mark 7, for about 20
minutes.

Cannelloni con ricotta e spinaci [F]
Cannelloni with Ricotta and Spinach

This dish freezes well – allow to cool completely, cover with foil, label and freeze.

Serves 6

4 *eggs for pasta*
65g *(2½ oz) grated*
  Parmesan cheese

For the filling
450g *(1 lb) spinach,*
  chopped
450g *(1 lb) fresh ricotta*
salt
freshly ground black
  pepper

a pinch of nutmeg
100g *(4 oz) grated*
  Parmesan cheese
2 *eggs, lightly beaten*

For the tomato sauce
2 397g *(14 oz) tins Italian*
  peeled tomatoes

salt
1 *beef stock cube*

For the white sauce
1 *tablespoon cornflour*
350ml *(12 fl oz) milk*

1 *teaspoon butter*
salt

Prepare the filling. Cook the spinach without any water, stirring often. Squeeze out any remaining water and chop again on a board or put it through a mincer. Mix with the ricotta, salt, pepper, nutmeg, Parmesan and the eggs.

Make your pasta (see page 144) and cut the strips into very large squares, the sides as large as the width of the rollers. Boil them in plenty of salted water and follow the same rules as for lasagne. Put a good amount of the filling into each cannellone, without sprinkling cheese on. Roll each one carefully, so that the filling does not come out, then place them in a buttered ovenproof dish, with a topping of Parmesan and a thin layer of white sauce on top.

To make the white sauce, dissolve the cornflour with 2 tablespoons of the milk. Put the rest of the milk in a saucepan over a moderate heat, with the butter and the salt. Bring to the boil and then mix with the dissolved cornflour, stirring continuously until it thickens. It should not be *too* thick, however. Pour this sauce on the cannelloni, spreading it evenly all over.

To make the tomato sauce, push the pulp of the tomatoes through a sieve, into a large saucepan, add salt and boil for 20 minutes. Add the stock cube diluted in 2 tablespoons of boiling water. Cover the cannelloni with this sauce, sprinkle with Parmesan cheese and bake in a preheated oven at 220°C (425°F), gas mark 7, for 20 minutes.

Cappelletti Ⓕ

Cappelletti are what in the shops you buy as tortellini; they have different names in different parts of Italy. Tortellini are all made by machine, while cappelletti are so called because their shape resembles a little hat, and cannot be made into this shape by machine.

You start by making the filling, which you can prepare the day before.

Serves 6–7 (Makes 350–400 cappelletti)

*homemade pasta made with
5 eggs (see page 144)
175g (6 oz) beef steak
175g (6 oz) chicken breast
100g (4 oz) lean pork
100g (4 oz) Italian salame
100g (4 oz) mortadella
65g (2½ oz) butter
salt*

*freshly ground black
pepper
½ teaspoon grated nutmeg
½ teaspoon ground
cinnamon
2 tablespoons grated
Parmesan cheese
1 egg, lightly beaten*

Grill the steak, the chicken breast, and the pork for a few minutes on each side. The meat does not need to be cooked completely. Cool, then mince the meat, *salame* and *mortadella*, and mix together. Melt the butter in a large saucepan over moderate heat, add the minced mixture and, stirring continuously, cook for 2–3 minutes. Add salt, pepper, nutmeg and cinnamon, mixing well, then the Parmesan and the egg. As soon as you add the egg, remove from the heat, and continue stirring until it is all well mixed and like a smooth paste.

Place this mixture into a basin, cover and refrigerate until you are ready to start making the cappelletti. Bring out of the fridge about 2 hours before use, or it will be stiff and hard and it will tear the fresh pasta.

Now make your pasta, making it a little softer than when making tagliatelle or lasagne. If you press two bits together when you roll it, they should stick.

When you have the first strip ready, rest it on a board and cut into squares with a very sharp knife. The classic way is to cut circles of pasta, but it is a very time-consuming process and in the cutting you will get many scraps which need recycling. So it is best to cut the pasta into 4cm (1½ inch) squares.

Put a little of the filling (a knob the size of a penny) into the middle of each square, fold diagonally, so you have a

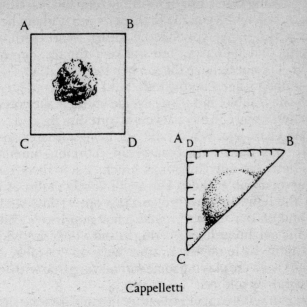

Cappelletti

Fold, bringing D to A. Press all around.

Twist B and C towards each other, and press the two points flat on top of one another.

triangle. Press the edges, then bring the two corners together one on top of the other and press lightly. The first cappelletto is now made and soon you will be an expert.

Sprinkle some flour on a tray and place the cappelletti on it as you make them. If you are going to freeze them, place the filled tray in the freezer for about 1 hour, then empty the contents of the tray into a freezer bag. Do not defrost cappelletti in advance; take them out only at cooking time or they will stick.

If you are going to use cappelletti within a couple of days after making, leave them on trays in a cool place. They will dry up, but do not worry; they will only require a little more cooking time. The main thing to avoid is letting the pasta dry up while you make them or you will not be able to stick the shapes around the filling. Work with small amounts of dough at a time and keep the rest covered in a bowl. Try not to have the kitchen too hot either. All this may sound rather a boring task, but I assure you, it is well worth the trouble. But if you decide not to make your own cappelletti, you can buy packets of tortellini instead.

Some years ago, when I did not have a freezer and my family was numerous, I made an enormous number of cappelletti for our Christmas lunch. I left them on the dining-room table, then I had to fill another table as well. I left the light on with the curtains open while we went out, and on our return I found a few inquisitive children from the neighbourhood peering in and wondering what on earth these little objects in lines were on my table. They thought we were playing some sort of war game with extra-terrestrial toy soldiers!

You can serve cappelletti either in soup or *asciutti* (dry), which means without broth, and with some kind of a sauce. It is best to cook them first in the same way, no matter how you are going to serve them, because they need a lot of cooking. If you boil them directly in the broth, you would need such a lot of it as it evaporates a great deal.

Dissolve 1 beef stock cube (2 if you have more than 250 cappelletti) in a large saucepan of water over high heat. Use chicken cubes if you have cappelletti in broth. Add a little salt, but not too much because the cubes are already quite salty. When the water boils, drop in the cappelletti, stirring occasionally. Spike the middle of one with a fork to see if it is tender (push the prongs where the pasta is folded). You must make sure that they are well cooked in the middle.

Cappelletti in brodo
Cappelletti in Broth as Soup

350ml (11 fl oz) stock
30–40 cappelletti per
  person

salt
grated Parmesan cheese

Have ready some stock of your choice (chicken or turkey stock is best to go with cappelletti). At Christmas, capon broth is recommended (see page 85). When you have boiled the cappelletti, drain the cooking water and add boiling broth, about 2–2½ ladles per person. Check the salt. Serve this soup with a little grated Parmesan.

Cappelletti alla panna
Cappelletti with Cream

Serves 4

200–220 cappelletti
80g (3 oz) butter
125ml (¼ pint) double
  cream

80g (3 oz) grated Parmesan
  cheese

Cook cappelletti as on page 160, then drain them into a warmed serving dish. Add the butter, cut up in shreds, and mix it in well. Pour in the cream, then put everything back into the saucepan. Heat well and quickly, stirring carefully with a wooden spoon. Keep the saucepan on the heat just long enough to warm the cream. Tip the contents back into a serving dish, or make individual portions, and add grated Parmesan cheese.

Cappelletti al ragù
Cappelletti with Meat and Tomato Sauce

Serves 4

Make a *ragù* sauce as on page 146. Cook 200–220 cappelletti (page 157), drain the cooking water, and tip them into a large warmed serving dish. Mix with some of the *ragù* and cheese, mix again, add the rest of the *ragù* and cheese, mix again, add the rest of the *ragù* and sprinkle more Parmesan cheese on top.

Lasagne [Ⓕ]

When you prepare lasagne, always make the sauce first.

Serves 6

3 large eggs for pasta
300g (12 oz) grated Parmesan cheese
1 tablespoon cornflour

about 350g (14 oz) plain flour
150ml (¼ pint) milk
1 teaspoon butter

For the sauce
450g (1 lb) stewing steak
1 medium-sized onion, peeled and chopped
100g (4 oz) margarine
1 medium-sized carrot, chopped
1 stick of celery, chopped

5–6 chopped fresh basil leaves or a pinch of dry basil
3 397g (14 oz) tins Italian peeled tomatoes
2 tablespoons tomato purée

Make pasta as explained on page 144. Lay the pasta strips to dry and then cut them into rectangular shapes roughly 10×6.5cm (4×2½ inches). Have a large saucepan of water ready on the stove. Bring it to the boil, add the salt and pop in the lasagne one by one, being very careful that they do not stick to each other. It helps to stir them continuously. Boil them for 2 minutes, then lift them out with a slotted spoon into a bowl containing cold water. If any are sticking, now is the time to separate them carefully with your fingers, while still in the cold water. Remove the pasta from the water one by one, and spread them out on a clean cloth.

Cook the sauce as for *ragù*, page 146. When you have minced the meat, do not put it back into the sauce. Put it in a basin, add 2 ladles of the sauce and 1 ladle of boiling water and mix thoroughly. If you used minced meat (which I don't advise unless you can't avoid it), strain the sauce at this point, remove the meat and proceed as above. This meat is the filling for the lasagne, while you use the sauce for the top layers.

Spread out all the pieces of lasagne, sprinkle some Parmesan cheese on each one, then put a teaspoon of meat in the middle of each piece of pasta. Roll them over and arrange them in an ovenproof dish, approximately 25×20×7.5cm (10×8×3 inch), lined with some of the sauce on the bottom. (Do not sprinkle cheese in the base of the dish as it will stick.) When you have arranged the first layer, sprinkle over a good amount of cheese and sauce, then make a second layer, and so on until you have used up all the ingredients. Do not fill the dish right to the top – leave about 1cm (½ inch). If the eggs are very large, it is sometimes difficult to judge exactly how much pasta you will make, but if you have any lasagne left, make up another small dish. Bake in a preheated oven at 190°C (375°F), gas mark 5, for 45 minutes, then increase the temperature to 220°C (430°F), gas mark 8 to brown the top.

To Freeze Lasagne

You can freeze lasagne as soon as you have finished layering the pasta, or after you have added the white sauce. Some people say the sauce is better if not frozen, but I have tried both ways and it tastes exactly the same to me.

Allow to cool completely, then cover it with foil, label and pop it into the freezer. I make about 20 eggs of lasagne at a time, so there is always some for unexpected visitors. There is no need to defrost it either: cook it in a preheated oven at 150°C (300°F), gas mark 2 for 1 hour, then proceed with the normal cooking time.

Instead of an ovenproof dish, you may like to use foil containers to cut down on washing up. In Britain women are very lucky indeed to have men who help with the washing up. In Italy the only task that some men will undertake is cooking for a party, which they do just to show off because it is an eccentric thing to do. But they usually require the wife's help in the most menial chores that go hand in hand with the actual cooking. I am unlucky in this respect because, although my husband is British, he never attempted to interfere with my Italian upbringing which made me accept the fact that the kitchen was only for women. Rather than shatter my beliefs, he provided me with a dishwasher very early on in our married life.

Tagliatelle Ⓕ

Prepare the sauce of your choice. Make pasta as explained on page 144. Let the strips dry until the pieces do not stick if you place one on top of another. Cut the length of each strip in sections of roughly 45cm (18 inches), but if you have trouble in managing long pasta, cut the sections to about 30cm (12 inches) long. Add the blade to the machine and put the strips through. After they are cut, spread them out on a cloth. If you have made pasta a few hours before your meal, cover the tagliatelle with another cloth. Keep them on a tray in a cool room and take great care when you lift them up to cook them. They break easily if too dry, so it is best to lift the cloth they are spread on and take it to the boiling pan.

For tagliatelle, the recipe is one egg per person and one extra. I personally think one egg is enough, without adding the extra one, but if you can eat large portions or if you are going to have this dish for your main course, then do the same as when you make tea: one per person and one for the pot!

When you have strained the tagliatelle, tip them into a large dish, add grated Parmesan cheese on top, and mix well. Pour on some of the sauce you will have prepared in advance (make it very hot), and mix again. Have some grated Parmesan in a dish and let your guests help themselves to a little extra on top.

You can freeze tagliatelle. If you have any leftovers mixed with the sauce, put them in a foil container and cover, label and freeze. Or make a thin layer of white sauce to cover the top. When you want to use them, follow the instructions for frozen lasagne (page 164). This dish is called *pasta al forno* (baked pasta).

Ravioli Ⓕ

Ravioli is a dish for Easter, as the filling is made up with fresh spinach and ricotta. In these days, when everything is available at any time of the year, it is not a problem to obtain the ingredients whenever you want to make this speciality.

If you cannot obtain ricotta, you can use cottage cheese, although I cannot guarantee that the taste will be the same.

Serves 4–5

3 eggs for pasta
about 350g (14 oz) plain
 flour

1 egg white for brushing on
 the strips

For the filling
175g (6 oz) cleaned spinach
225g (8 oz) ricotta
1 egg, lightly beaten
salt

freshly ground black pepper
a pinch of cinnamon
50g (2 oz) grated Parmesan
 cheese

To make the filling, cook the spinach in a saucepan, without adding any water, stirring often. When cooked, squeeze out any surplus moisture and chop it up very finely. Mix it with ricotta, blending well together. Add the egg to the mixture, with the salt and pepper, the cinnamon and Parmesan. Leave this mixture in a basin and cover it with a cloth.

Now make pasta the usual way (page 144), rolling one strip at a time and making it the same consistency as for lasagne. Lay the first strip on a floured cloth on the table, put small amounts (a teaspoon or so) of the filling in straight lines on the strip of pasta, in the middle of imaginary 4cm (1½ inch) squares (see illustration), going up to half the length of the strip. Quickly and lightly brush the second half of the strip with the egg, then carefully lift it over the half with the filling. Press with the tip of your fingers all around each knob of filling, pricking carefully with a fork if there is any air trapped in. Using a pastry cutter, cut into squares.

Leave the ravioli on a floured board or cloth while you

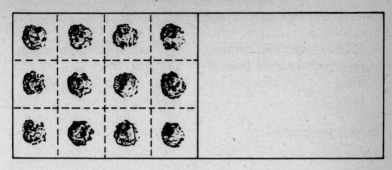

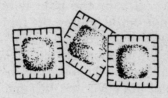

Ravioli

Brush the blank side with egg white, then lift over the other side,
pressing down along the imaginary lines.

Press sides of ravioli with the prongs of a fork.

prepare the remainder. If you are quick in your work, you
can make two strips of pasta at a time, one where you put
the pieces of filling all along and the other for the top.

You must be careful not to let the pasta dry during the
making process. Ravioli should be cooked straight away in
plenty of salted boiling water for about 10 minutes, but it
is always wise to try one to make sure it has boiled long
enough. Once cooked, drain ravioli on to a warmed serving
dish. You can freeze ravioli in the same way as cappelletti
(page 157).

You can serve ravioli with butter, cheese and cream or
with a meat and tomato sauce. A very good way of serving
ravioli is the following:

Serves 4–5

2 397g (14 oz) tins tomato
  juice or the pulp from 2
  397g (14 oz) tins peeled
  tomatoes
salt
freshly ground black
  pepper

75g (3 oz) grated Parmesan
  cheese
150ml (¼ pint) double
  cream

Boil the tomato juice or the pulp with salt, for 15–20 minutes. Keep hot while boiling the ravioli until tender. Season the juice with pepper and when you have drained the ravioli, pour the juice on top, mixing well, and add the grated Parmesan. Quickly heat the cream and pour it over. Do not mix again, but cover the dish and leave it in a hot place for about 10 minutes before taking it to the table.

Agnolotti Ⓕ

Agnolotti are like outsized cappelletti. The filling is the same as for ravioli (page 166), only with the addition of a pinch of nutmeg.

Cut the strips of pasta into very large squares (about 10cm/4 inches). Fill each square with a heaped tablespoon of the mixture and make them in the same way as cappelletti (page 157). You need 6–7 of these large agnolotti per person. For 4–5 portions make the same amount of filling as for ravioli, use 3 eggs for the pasta, and about 350g (14 oz) plain flour.

Vincisgrassi Ⓕ

In some Italian regions another name for lasagne is *vincisgrassi*. The only difference is that the squares of pasta are not rolled. Make the pasta and sauce in the same way as for lasagne (page 162). When you have minced the meat, mix it again with the sauce.

Boil the squares of pasta, then lay them on a cloth, in a heap, and mop up the surplus water with some kitchen paper. Make layers in an ovenproof dish in the same way as rolled lasagne. The ingredients are exactly the same but this dish is quicker to make. I only make *vincisgrassi* if I am pushed for time, because, when you have prepared everything, it seems a shame not to serve the classic lasagne dish.

Polenta

Polenta is to Italian peasants what potatoes are to the Irish. It is mostly a winter dish, something you know is going to fill you up and warm you as well. They say this dish is what gives Italian people their fiery temperament. My husband says it is probably because it gives them indigestion. Well, I can assure you that I have enjoyed polenta many a time without regretting it, and I hope you will too.

Italians living in the countryside will still eat polenta every day in the winter, and until some years ago it used to be cooked in a big cauldron on an open fire. Now it is cooked on more modern stoves, but the basic dish is still the same. The way peasants eat polenta differs from the way people in the towns would serve it. A large, long, scrubbed wooden slab, kept just for polenta and for pasta-making, would be laid on the kitchen table and the polenta tipped on it in one go, spread to the thickness of 1cm (½ inch), sprinkled generously with grated *pecorino* cheese on top, and sauce or perhaps just pieces of sausage spread all over.

The family would sit around the table, fork in hand, and they would eat the portion that was in front of them. I often cooked it in this way and my children used to love eating their way into the polenta by making maps of different countries. Some Italians will serve polenta on individual dishes and perhaps make two layers. As one who has had a chance of trying it from the board, I can assure you it is much tastier served only in one layer. So I suggest that you use large oval serving dishes, one for each person.

When you buy yellow maize flour, make sure you ask for the 'fine' type, because there is also a type looking rather like semolina, which is used by people in northern Italy for their polenta, and it is very different from the polenta I've described.

Serves 4

500g (17 oz) 'fine' yellow   *salt*
  maize flour
about 2.5 litres (4½ pints)
  water

Put the water in a large deep saucepan to heat. There must be a lot of room for stirring, so the water should not come up to more than half the side of the saucepan. When the water is hot, but before it reaches boiling point, add the flour, one handful at a time, with your left hand, while with your right hand you stir continuously, using a wooden spoon, or, better, a hand whisk (not electric).

Let the flour run through your fingers, like soft rain. There must be no lumps in the polenta and you only achieve this if you finish pouring in all the flour before the water boils. If, however, you still manage to make some lumps, remove them by pouring through a strainer and squashing them with the back of a spoon. While the polenta boils, be very careful, because it will splatter a lot. Keep the heat low and let it simmer gently for about 45 minutes, stirring frequently. A few minutes before it is ready, add the salt. Some of the polenta will stick to the bottom of the pan but that is to be expected; just keep stirring as it goes on cooking. When cooking time is over, there will be a crust around the pan which will start peeling off, and the polenta will be quite thick.

Pour it on to the large dishes you have prepared and spread it quickly with a wooden spoon, discarding the bit stuck at the bottom of the pan. Sprinkle a good quantity of grated *pecorino* cheese on top, together with the sauce you have prepared.

Sugo per polenta
Sauce for Polenta

Serves 4

Before starting to make polenta, it is best to prepare the sauce.

450g (1 lb) minced lean pork
1 medium-sized onion, peeled and chopped
2 tablespoons olive oil
6 rashers unsmoked streaky rindless bacon, diced

salt
freshly ground black pepper
2 397g (14 oz) tins peeled tomatoes (optional)
125g (5 oz) grated pecorino cheese

You can cut the meat in small cubes, if you prefer. Fry the onion in the oil until soft, then add the bacon and cook it very slowly to draw the maximum amount of juice from it. Add the meat and continue cooking gently, then season. When the meat is nearly cooked, check the amount of juice you have in the pan, because you must judge if there is enough to spread over a plate of polenta for the number of portions. If you think there is not much liquid, add the strained tomatoes and boil for 20 more minutes. Serve, sprinkled with *pecorino* cheese.

Sugo con salsicce
Italian Sausage Sauce

Serves 4

1 medium-sized onion,
  peeled and chopped
4 rashers unsmoked bacon,
  diced
4 Italian sausages,
  chopped

2 tablespoons olive oil
2 397g (14 oz) tins
  tomatoes, drained

Fry the onion, bacon and sausage in the olive oil, then add the tomatoes and simmer for 20–25 minutes.

    Other ways of serving polenta are:
with ragù sauce (page 146)
with Italian sausages and bacon (page 154)
with duck (page 232)
with game (pages 228,238)

Polenta al baccalà
Polenta with Dried Cod

Baccalà is dried, salted cod. Don't be put off by the look of it when you go to buy it, because it looks quite different once you have prepared it. Get a piece cut from a large fish, not the small fillets you can get in packets.

Serves 4

450g (1 lb) dried cod	*4–5 celery leaves, chopped*
3 tablespoons olive oil	*1 sprig of parsley*
1 medium-sized onion,	*2 397g (14 oz) tins peeled*
peeled and sliced	*tomatoes, drained*

Soak the cod for 3 days in enough water to cover it, changing the water each day. Cut it into pieces 5cm (2 inches) square, removing the bones at the same time. Usually it is filleted, but it is best to make sure.

Heat the oil in a large saucepan with the onion, celery leaves and parsley. Cook until the onion is soft, then add the tomatoes. Simmer for 10 minutes, then add the pieces of cod and continue simmering for 1 hour.

The sauce should be thick enough to be spread on the polenta without being runny. Check if it needs any salt (remember the cod was salted). Flake the pieces of fish on top of the portions of polenta and spread the sauce evenly. No grated cheese is required with this sauce.

Pizza

There is no need for an introduction to pizza, which everybody knows. *Pizza napoletana*, although it originated in Naples, has become the pizza of many regions, as in different places it has a different garnish and filling and then takes the name of the place. The basic dough is the same, no matter what name you give it.

Serves 4

15g (½ oz) fresh yeast   salt
350g (14 oz) plain flour

Mix the yeast with 2 tablespoons warm water, leave it for a few minutes until frothy, then mix with the flour, adding more water if necessary and a little salt. Make it into a soft dough, and knead it until smooth and elastic. Put it in a basin, cover it with a cloth and leave it in a warm place for 2–2½ hours.

When the dough has risen, roll it out on a lightly floured surface into a circular shape about 5mm (¼ inch) thick. Place it in a greased baking tin and with your hands spread it out, pushing the sides out, making a higher ridge all the way round. With the tips of your fingers, make little depressions on the dough.

Pizza al pomodoro
Pizza with Tomatoes

Serves 4

a few drops olive oil
350g (12 oz) fresh, very ripe
  tomatoes
150g (6 oz) mozzarella or
  any soft cheese, cubed
50g (2 oz) anchovy fillets,
  chopped

green and black olives,
  stoned and halved
a few capers
a pinch of oregano
a small piece pimento
  (optional)

Prepare the pizza base as in the previous recipe. Sprinkle a few drops of olive oil on the top of the dough, then arrange the rest of the ingredients on the top. Bake it in a preheated oven at 220–230°C (425–440°F), gas mark 7–8, for about 20–25 minutes.

Pizza alle cipolle
Onion Pizza

Serves 4

2 tablespoons olive oil
2 large onions, peeled and
  sliced
salt

freshly ground black
  pepper
fresh chopped rosemary
  leaves

Prepare the pizza base (see page 174). Heat the olive oil and fry onions until soft, adding a little salt. Remove the onions with a slotted spoon and spread them over the dough. Sprinkle with a little more oil, some pepper and a good amount of rosemary. Press them down gently with your fingers and bake as in previous recipe.

5

Pesce
Fish

During Holy Week a lot of fish is eaten because people respect the fasting of the last few days of Lent, especially Good Friday. On the Thursday, which is Holy (Maundy) Thursday, a visit is made to the Holy Sepulchre: nearly all the churches have a scene depicting the tomb where Jesus was buried, and it is customary for the place to be decorated with lots of plants grown in pots especially for this occasion: wheat, barley and other cereals which have been sown and kept all the time in a dark room, so they consist of a mass of whitish thin shoots, which have grown so tall that they cascade down. On Good Friday in southern Italy, they have a procession 'of the dead Christ', when they carry these pots shoulder high. It really is an unusual and strange sight.

During these days only fish will be eaten – no meat will be consumed – but all the time preparations are being made for the Easter festival. On the Saturday, the sign for the end of Lent is given by the joyful peal of the bells of all the churches, St Peter's in Rome giving the lead (the bells do not ring during the time of Christ's death). After that you can eat anything you like, and the ribbons from the trunks of the fruit trees in the garden (which were tied at the same time as the bells were stopped from tolling) can be untied. If you follow this custom your trees will give you plentiful fruit.

'*Si tira la rete*' ('The net is being pulled in') somebody shouts on the beach and a crowd of men, women and children will be drawn to the water's edge in the general excitement to see the pulling in of the nets. It is a pastime, on the sandy beaches of the Adriatic coast, to go in the early morning to the harbour or to the beach to wait for the day's catch. Usually the older fishermen and their wives will pull the nets ashore, while the more able ones go further afield and stay out fishing all night. The nets are thrown into the sea during the night, or in the evening, and in the morning they will be pulled to the shore. Two small boats will bring the ends to the beach, while the middle part will still be a long way out.

Being pulled and pulled, in a rhythmic movement, accompanied by singing, the big net is gradually brought nearer and you can follow its progress by watching the movement of the corks floating on the top. When the main part of the net is very near the shore, the sides will come together and in a last effort, the middle and largest part of the net will be pulled in. This is where the fish have been trapped.

Mullet, needles, sardines, crabs, squid, mackerel, whiting, sole, cockles and all sorts of small shells are being caught this way. The children will be there in force, with their buckets filled with water, to catch the very small ones that either the fishermen do not bother to take or that escape from the net. You have to be quick if you want to buy some there and then, because all the fish will be sorted out in no time and taken to the market or to restaurants. If you manage to get some, it is a real treat to be able to cook it straight away. The best way to treat it is to make a *frittura mista* (a mixed fry-up).

Clean all the fish, take off all the heads, pull out the interiors, cut fins and tails. Wash it all well, and drain it. Sprinkle it with salt, dip it in a bowl of flour and see that every fish is well coated. Put a good amount of frying oil in a large frying pan and heat it. When sizzling, drop in the fish, putting together the ones of the same species. Move the pan, rocking it gently from side to side as you fry, and after a few minutes, turn the fish on the other side. When it is golden on both sides, lift the fish with a slice and place it on a dish where you have spread some white kitchen paper. Serve it at once with a sprinkle of lemon juice, accompanied by a green salad and crusty bread.

Baccalà al forno
Oven-Baked Dried Cod

Serves 4

600g (1¼ lb) dried cod
2 tablespoons parsley,
  chopped
½ clove garlic, chopped

100ml (3½ fl oz) olive oil
freshly ground black
  pepper
juice of 1 lemon

Prepare the cod as described on page 173. Cut the fish into 4 portions. Place in a greased ovenproof dish. Mix the parsley and garlic together with the oil, then pour over the fish, adding a little pepper. Cook in a preheated oven at 200°C (400°F), gas mark 6, for 30 minutes. Be careful not to break the pieces of fish. Squeeze the lemon juice over the fish before serving.

Baccalà arrosto
Roast Cod

Serves 4

600g (1¼ lb) dried cod
2 tablespoons fresh chopped
  parsley
½ clove garlic, chopped
2 tablespoons olive oil

50g (2 oz) fresh white
  breadcrumbs
4 tablespoons milk

Prepare the cod as described on page 173. Cut the fish into 4 portions. Mix the parsley and garlic with the olive oil and the breadcrumbs. Place the fish in an ovenproof dish and spread this mixture on top of every piece. Pour the milk over it and cover. Bake in a preheated oven at 180°C (350°F), gas mark 4, for 30 minutes, then take off the lid and let the top crispen for 10 minutes at 220°C (425°F), gas mark 7.

Brodetto
Seafood Soup

A typical dish from *L'amarissimo*, the Adriatic, the most bitter of the seas. This is a dish best made for a number of persons, because you need as many different types of fish as you can get. In fact the experts say that the right number of varieties required is 13, but I assure you that one can make a very tasty *brodetto* with half that number.

Serves 6

2kg (4 lb) fish: a mixture of cod, plaice, sole, shrimps, prawns, squid, cockles, mussels, lobster (optional), trout, eel, mullet (any fish that you can get will add more flavour to the dish)

150ml (5 fl oz) olive oil

2 onions, peeled and thinly sliced

450g (1 lb) very ripe tomatoes, skinned, seeded and chopped

2 tablespoons chopped fresh parsley

a few celery leaves, chopped

100ml (3½ fl oz) white wine

1 garlic clove

salt

freshly ground black pepper

slices brown toast, to serve

Clean all the fish, gutting and tailing, but leaving as many heads as you can. Take the dorsal bone out of the squid, pull out the mouth and eyes, scrape the mussels and cockles and put them in a large saucepan. Cover and cook for a few minutes at moderate heat, shaking the pan until the mussels and cockles open. Wash all the fish. Heat the oil in a large saucepan and cook the onions until soft. Add the tomatoes, parsley and celery leaves and cook for 10 minutes. Pour in the wine and season with garlic, salt and pepper. Cook for 15 minutes uncovered, then discard the garlic. Add the fish, in pieces, starting with the species that take longer to cook, then wait a little longer and add the rest. Pour in enough water to come about 2.5cm (1 inch) over the fish. Cover, bring to the boil and cook for 20 minutes. The water should by then be level with the fish. Remove the pan from the heat and leave to rest, covered, for 10 minutes. Line individual plates with slices of toast. With a ladle, pour some of the liquid on each piece of toast, before placing the fish on top. Serve with some crusty bread and salad of your choice.

Anguilla fritta
Fried Eel

Eel is a dish for Christmas Eve. The type sought for is called *capitone*, which is a large type of eel. To skin an eel, make a circular incision at the base of the head, hang it on a hook and carefully start peeling off the skin where you have made the cut. As soon as you can get hold of some skin, just pull and it will come off easily, holding it with a cloth, right down to the tip of the tail. Cut the head off.

Pesce

Serves 4

500g (17 oz) eel
salt
freshly ground black
  pepper

fresh sage and bay leaves
flour
oil for frying
lemon wedges for serving

Cut the eel into pieces about 2.5cm (1 inch) thick. Wash these well. Season. Wash as many sage leaves and bay leaves as you have pieces of eel. Push a toothpick through each piece of fish to hold one sage leaf on one side and a bay leaf on the other. Roll the piece in flour.

Heat the oil in a frying pan and fry the eel, turning once or twice, until golden. Drain on kitchen paper and serve hot with lemon wedges.

Anguilla arrosto
Roast Eel

Serves 4

500g (17 oz) eel, cleaned
100ml (3½ fl oz) olive oil
juice of 1 lemon
40g (1½ oz) fresh white
  breadcrumbs

2–3 chopped fresh bay
  leaves, plus extra for
  roasting
salt
freshly ground black
  pepper

Cut the eel into pieces about 5cm (2 inches) long. Prepare a marinade with the olive oil, lemon juice, breadcrumbs and the bay leaves. Mix all these ingredients together. Season the eel with salt and pepper and marinate for 1½ hours.

Remove the eel pieces from the marinade with a slotted spoon and arrange the pieces on long skewers. Alternate each piece of eel with a bay leaf, then pour over the marinade. Place the skewers on a tin so that the fish does not touch the surface. Roast in a preheated oven at 160°C (325°F), gas mark 3, for 40 minutes, basting frequently.

Triglie al tegame
Mullet Casserole

Serves 4

*600g (1¼ lb) red mullet,
  cleaned and gutted
½ garlic clove, crushed
25g (1 oz) celery, chopped
2 tablespoons chopped
  parsley*

*100ml (3½ fl oz) olive oil
6 fresh pear-shaped
  tomatoes, skinned,
  seeded and chopped
salt
freshly ground black
  pepper*

Wash the mullet well in cold water. Mix the garlic, celery and parsley together. Heat the oil in a saucepan and cook the garlic mixture until golden. Add the tomatoes and cook for 15 minutes, stirring occasionally. Then add the fish, season, cover and cook for a further 30 minutes.

Scampi con riso
Prawns with Rice

Serves 4

50g (2 oz) margarine
1 medium-sized onion,
  peeled and chopped
2 tablespoons plain flour
200ml (7 fl oz) white wine
400ml (14 fl oz) milk

200g (7 oz) tin peeled
  tomatoes, drained
275g (10 oz) fresh or frozen
  prawns
400g (15 oz) rice

Melt the margarine in a large saucepan and cook the onion until tender. Mix the flour in a little of the wine, and add it to the onion with the rest of the wine. Stir and pour in the milk with the pulp of the strained tomatoes. Reduce the heat, add the prawns and simmer for 30 minutes. Meanwhile, rinse the rice and place it in a saucepan with enough water to come about 2.5cm (1 inch) above it. Bring it to the boil and simmer it for about 15 minutes. Drain the rice, divide it into portions and serve with the hot prawns.

Salmì
Salmi of Fish

Serves 4

500g (17 oz) fish, such as
  sprats, mackerel, cod and
  haddock
3 tablespoons olive oil
½ clove garlic, crushed
2 tablespoons fresh chopped
  parsley

2 tablespoons fresh chopped
  sage
juice of 1 lemon
salt
freshly ground black
  pepper

Fillet the fish first. If you have large fillets, cut them up into pieces. Heat the oil in a large saucepan with all the other ingredients, except the lemon juice. Cook for 5 minutes, then add the lemon juice and the pieces of fish. Season with salt and pepper. Simmer for about 30 minutes, until the fish flakes easily, adding a very small amount of water if the sauce gets too dry. Stir often.

Sogliole al vino
Sole in Wine

With a knife, ease out a bit of the skin at the tail end, on the dark side. Pull up enough to be able to hold it between two fingers. Now, with a cloth in your other hand, hold the fish firmly on the table and holding that bit of skin, pull it all off decisively and quickly. Do the same on the other side. Maybe your fishmonger will do this for you, but it doesn't take long.

Serves 4

4 large sole	1 medium-sized onion
salt	25g (1 oz) margarine
freshly ground black pepper	2 bay leaves
4 knobs of butter or margarine for spreading	15g (½ oz) fresh chopped parsley
	200ml (7 fl oz) white wine

Wash the sole and dry them with kitchen paper. Sprinkle with salt and pepper and spread a little butter or margarine on each one of them.

Grease an ovenproof dish large enough to accommodate the sole in one layer. Heat the margarine in a large saucepan and cook the onion until tender. Add the bay leaves and parsley. Mix well, then add the wine, and boil for a few moments. Pour this sauce over the fish and bake in a preheated oven at 210°C (420°F), gas mark 6–7, for 25 minutes.

Calamari ripieni
Stuffed Squid

Serves 4

1kg (2 lb) squid
salt
2 tablespoons fresh chopped parsley
5–6 fresh chopped basil leaves
a sprig of fennel, chopped

1 clove garlic, crushed
50g (2 oz) fresh white breadcrumbs
4 tablespoons olive oil
margarine

Clean the fish, removing the eyes, mouth and the dorsal bone. Peel the large sac, scrape the tentacles. Wash it well, dry it with a towel and sprinkle with salt. Mix together parsley, basil, fennel and garlic, then mix with the breadcrumbs and olive oil. Divide this mixture between the number of squid and stuff each one.

Grease an ovenproof dish big enough to take the squid side by side in one layer, then place a small knob of margarine on top of each one. Cover and bake in a preheated oven at 180°C (350°F), gas mark 4, for at least 1 hour. Some need more time to cook than others, so it is best to test if the flesh is tender with a fork. Then remove the lid and bake for 5 more minutes at 220°C (425°F), gas mark 7.

Calamaretti fritti
Fried Baby Squid

Serves 4

Buy the very small tender squid. Clean them by removing the soft bone (you can push it off at the pointed end). Remove the eyes, the mouth or beak, clean inside the sac, and scrape the tentacles. Cut them in slices, so they will look like rings. Wash them well under running water, then drain them and mop up the moisture with a paper towel. Sprinkle salt on the pieces, then roll them in flour. Prepare a frying pan of hot oil with a cover because they will splatter, then fry them until golden on both sides. Serve with slices of lemon, crusty bread and a salad.

Calamaretti alla marchigiana
Baby Squid the Marchigiana Way

Serves 6

100ml (3 fl oz) olive oil
½ clove garlic, crushed
2 tablespoons fresh chopped parsley
1 kg (2 lb) squid, cleaned
salt
2 anchovy fillets, chopped

1 small piece pimento, chopped
200ml (7 fl oz) white wine
100ml (3½ fl oz) water
fried bread or toast, to serve

In a large saucepan over moderate heat, heat the oil and the garlic. Remove the garlic as soon as it starts colouring, then add the parsley. Add the fish, stirring. Sprinkle with some salt and add the anchovy fillets and pimento. (If you do not like pimento, substitute it with freshly ground black pepper.) Cook quickly for a few moments, then add the wine and continue cooking until it evaporates.

Now lower the heat, add the water and cover, leaving the fish to simmer and cook slowly. When tender, arrange the *calamaretti* in a serving dish with fried bread or slices of toast.

Stoccafisso all'anconetana
Dried Cod the Ancona Way

Unlike *baccalà* (see page 173), *stoccafisso* is not salted, just dried in the air.

You can buy the fish already soaked, but if you buy it dry, it will need soaking in cold water for 4 days, changing the water twice a day.

Serves 4

1kg (2 lb) dried cod
salt
1 large onion, peeled and
   finely chopped
300ml (10½ fl oz) olive oil
rosemary, oregano and
   marjoram
2–3 sage leaves
1 stick celery, chopped
1 medium-sized carrot,
   chopped

1 pimento, chopped
1 clove garlic, crushed
397g (14 oz) tin peeled
   tomatoes, chopped
1 tablespoon tomato purée
5–6 green or black olives,
   stoned
1kg (2 lb) potatoes, peeled
   and sliced
milk

When soaked, remove the bones from the fish and cut into large pieces, then sprinkle them with salt. In a saucepan, fry the onion in two-thirds of the olive oil. When the onion is tender, add a pinch of rosemary, oregano, marjoram, the sage leaves, celery, carrot, pimento and garlic. Stir all these ingredients together, then pour in the tomatoes and the tomato purée, diluted in a little water. Cook for about 10 minutes.

Place a cooking rack at the bottom of a large casserole, and on top place a few pieces of the fish. On the first layer, pour over some of the sauce, and continue layering until all the fish and sauce are used. Add the olives. Peel the potatoes, wash and thickly slice and season with salt. Make a last layer with the potatoes. Pour on top the remaining olive oil and some milk, to cover the potatoes. Simmer for at least 2 hours. With the *sugo* (juice) you can make pasta or polenta (see pages 144, 169).

Tonno fresco
Fresh Tuna

Serves 6

1kg (2 lb) fresh tuna, in one piece
100ml (3½ fl oz) olive oil
1 small onion, peeled and quartered
salt
freshly ground black pepper
juice of 1 lemon

Soak the fish in water for about 20 minutes. Put in a large saucepan with the oil and the onion. Cook, turning it a few times, for 30 minutes. Add salt and pepper and enough water to cover the fish. Cover and bring to the boiling point, then simmer for a further hour. When ready, lift it out and cut it into slices. You can serve it hot, just squeezing some lemon juice on it, or you can leave it to cool to serve it cold.

For the cold dish, here is a sauce to accompany it:

½ clove garlic, peeled and crushed (optional)
1 tablespoon fresh chopped parsley
2 anchovy fillets, chopped

1 tablespoon capers, chopped
2 tablespoons olive oil
juice of ½ lemon

Mix together the garlic, parsley, anchovies and capers to make a paste. Mix with the oil and lemon juice and, with a spoon, cover the top of each piece of fish.

Tonno fresco al pomodoro
Tuna with Tomato

This recipe is for tuna fish, but you can also cook other fish, such as cod, haddock and halibut, this way.

Serves 6

1kg (2 lb) fresh tuna, cleaned and sliced
salt
freshly ground black pepper
flour
100ml (3½ fl oz) olive oil
½ onion, peeled and chopped

2 anchovy fillets, chopped
2 tablespoons fresh chopped parsley
100ml (3½ fl oz) white wine
2 tablespoons tomato purée
1 tablespoon water
½ bay leaf, chopped

Season the tuna and coat with pieces of flour. Place the oil in a saucepan, and brown in it the pieces of fish, turning them once. Lift them out with a slotted spoon. Add onion, anchovies and parsley to the oil. Stir for a few moments, then pour in the wine and cook quickly. Mix the tomato purée with the water and add it to the pan, together with the bay leaf and a little salt and pepper. Cook for about 30 minutes. Add the fish and simmer for a further 15 minutes. Serve hot.

Tonno con piselli
Tuna and Fresh Peas

Serves 4

1 medium-sized onion, peeled and chopped
1 medium-sized carrot, chopped
a few celery leaves, chopped
60g (2¼ oz) butter
500g (17 oz) fresh peas, shelled

397g (14 oz) tin peeled tomatoes or 8 pear-shaped tomatoes, skinned and chopped
salt
freshly ground black pepper
184g (6½ oz) tin tuna

Cook the chopped vegetables in the butter until tender, stirring often. Then add the peas and tomatoes, salt and pepper. Stir well, and after 5 minutes add the tuna with the oil from the tin. Cover and simmer for a further 40 minutes.

6

Carne

Meat

More and more people like lean meat, but there are times when I wish there was more fat on it, as there was in wartime, when we even had to make soap with our scraps. We had forgotten what a piece of beef was like: we used to get small amounts of lamb or pork shared with some farmer. The rationing system broke down in Italy as soon as it was started and, in a typical Italian way, everything was chaos. 'Help yourself' was the general attitude and you were able to eat if you had something to exchange for what you needed. A lot of bartering went on, and we considered ourselves lucky if we were in contact with some farmers. I used to give one loaf of bread in return for having my hair done.

One day lots of people clubbed together to buy a young

ox from a farmer to be able to have some beef. Who would kill it, and how? Nobody was an expert and there were no weapons available. Somebody in the village may have had a shotgun, but this would have attracted the attention of some pro-Germans who could shop us for possessing firearms. A man who was a caretaker in the priest's house (there was no priest in the village) said he had some experience in butchering. In fact, he had started to buy the odd lamb or pig which he then sold by the kilogram. Did he know the difference in strength between a pig or lamb and an ox? He said he could do it, although we later found out that this self-appointed butcher was in fact a cobbler. To avoid making a mess of somebody's stable, it was decided that the improvised abattoir should be in the open air, near a tree, where the animal could be tied up. Its horns were strapped to the trunk of the tree and then Severino appeared with his weapon, an old wood chopper.

All the people gathered to see the spectacle; someone might think of us as cruel and insensitive, but in those days you had to get your priorities right and the first thing we all aimed for was general survival. Also, seeing many people killed in very gruesome circumstances must have hardened our feelings.

And so, down came Severino's blow in the middle of the poor beast's head, but the cobbler – as well as being no butcher – was lame, unsteady on his feet and short, so his blow did not make a great impact against the strength of the ox, which, with a powerful jerk and a howl, freed himself from the ropes and ran amok amongst us with the axe stuck in his head. No bomb could have caused more panic! I found myself climbing a drainpipe to reach safety through an open window. But it all ended well. The ox fell into a ditch and some farmers got hold of the rope still attached to his horns and finished off the unfortunate animal, which was to be our food and soap for the time being.

Vitellone arrosto
Pot-Roasted Beef

Vitellone is a young ox. *Rosbif*, with an accent on the 'o', is supposed to be what in Britain is called roast beef. It is in fact different both in its look and taste because Italian meat has hardly any fat on it, so you have to add fat when cooking. A popular way to treat it is to add some *lardelli* (little pieces of lard). Make small holes in it with the point of a knife and push in the pieces of lard or fat from slices of bacon. These *lardelli* will help to keep the meat tender and moist while cooking.

Italian housewives are very fond of pot roasting. Some friends of mine, visiting England, were horrified when I went out with them leaving a joint in the oven, saying it would be cooked by the time we came back. 'Without keeping an eye on it?' They have to keep looking at their meat or it will be too dry, or tough or burned. They cannot understand that meat does not need any attention while roasting, if you have prepared it properly and leave it at the right temperature.

There is no need to add *lardelli* to the meat unless you are pot roasting a very lean piece of meat. When I want to cook meat this way, I buy a piece of topside and ask my butcher not to prepare it for roasting. I cut off most of the fat attached to the meat and tie the piece with string, so it will keep its shape.

Serves 6

1.25kg (2½ lb) topside
 beef
fat from 4 slices bacon
salt
freshly ground black
 pepper
a few marjoram leaves
a sage sprig

a rosemary sprig
100ml (3½ fl oz) olive oil
1 clove garlic
1 small whole onion
200ml (7 fl oz) white wine
1 beef cube dissolved in
 300ml (½ pint) boiling
 water

For the gravy
1 tablespoon flour   150ml (¼ pint) water

Make some holes in the meat about 5cm (2 inches) apart,
and push in the squares of fat which you have prepared,
first rolling them in salt and pepper. Wash and clean the
herbs and push a few small pieces into the holes as well.
Put the oil in a casserole, add the meat and cook quickly
to brown all over, turning it a few times. Season with salt
and pepper, add the garlic, onion and herbs, and after 5
more minutes, the wine. Lower the heat, cover and cook
very slowly. Make stock in a basin with the beef cube and
water. Turn the meat often, adding a little of the stock
every now and then. Cook for at least 2–2½ hours. Try it
by pushing a long needle in: the needle should go in easily
and the juice that comes out should be free of blood. Lift
out the meat, cover with foil and keep hot. Skim the fat
from the top of the cooking liquid with a spoon, add the
water to the pan, mix well with a wooden spoon, then
strain it. Return it to the pan, mix the flour with 2
tablespoons water, stir it into the gravy without any
lumps, bring to the boil and boil for 1 minute. Serve with
the roast.

Vitellone arrosto marinato
Marinated Roast Beef

An alternative to this way of roasting is to marinate the joint in red wine before cooking. Prepare in the same way, add *lardelli*, then mix all the washed and chopped herbs with red, not white, wine. Pour all this on the meat and leave it covered for 6–7 hours or overnight. Cook it with oil in the same way as above, then season it and pour the marinade over.

Vitellone marinato o 'alla zingara'
Marinade of Beef or Beef 'the Gipsy Way'

Serves 6–7

1kg (2 lb) beef (topside or any cut suitable for roasting, as long as it is tender and lean)
salt
sage and rosemary leaves

3 tablespoons olive oil
juice of 1½ lemons
freshly ground black pepper
50g (2 oz) Cheddar cheese, shredded

Prepare the meat, cutting off any fat. If you had to remove the string for taking the fat off, tie the joint again with some cotton, so it will keep its shape and be easier to cut. Sprinkle the joint with salt, wrap in foil, together with some washed sage and rosemary leaves. Roast in a preheated oven for about 1 hour at 200°C (400°F), gas mark 6. Check that it is cooked on the outside, and that the flesh inside is pink red. When a skewer is inserted into the centre, the juice that comes out should be pink red.

Leave to cool, remove the foil, then slice the meat very thinly. Arrange the slices on a large serving dish. Make one layer, then mix the olive oil with the lemon juice, adding some pepper. Spoon this on top of the meat, making sure you put some on each slice. Make another layer of meat and repeat the process. (If there is not enough liquid, depending on how many slices of meat you have managed to make, make a little more.) On top of the second layer, sprinkle the shredded cheese. Cover the dish with foil, put in the fridge and leave it for at least 1 hour before serving. Accompany it with a green salad or mixed vegetables.

Vitellone al forno
Roast Beef

Serves 6–7

2kg (4½ lb) sirloin, topside or silverside, trimmed
fat from 4 rashers of bacon
salt
freshly ground black pepper
100ml (3 fl oz) olive oil

1 small onion, peeled and chopped
1 stick of celery, chopped
1 small carrot, chopped
2 tablespoons chopped fresh parsley

For the gravy
1 tablespoon cornflour
100ml (3 fl oz) fortified wine, such as Marsala, 'Vin Santo' or sherry

300ml (½ pint) water

Tie the joint so it keeps its shape during cooking, and insert *lardelli* (see page 195). In pre-foil days, this dish would be cooked in a covered pan – now you can place it in foil, season, pour the oil on top with the vegetables, close the foil tightly around it and cook in a preheated oven for 3 hours at 180°C (350°F), gas mark 3–4. When ready, lift the joint out of the foil and place the juice in the roasting tin. Skim off the fat. Cover the meat again with the foil and keep it hot.

Mix 1 tablespoon cornflour with 'Vin Santo' (holy wine) or Marsala or sherry. Pour the water into the roasting tin, mix well with a wooden spoon, strain, return to the tin, then add the dissolved cornflour. Bring it gently to the boil, stirring all the time. Slice the meat, arrange on a serving dish and pour the sauce over the top.

Salsa italiana Ⓕ
Italian Sauce

This is another delicious sauce to be served with roast beef.

1 tablespoon olive oil
1 medium-sized onion,
 peeled and chopped
100ml (3 fl oz) white wine
100g (4 oz) mushrooms,
 thinly sliced

a sprig of thyme
1 bay leaf, chopped
300ml (½ pint) stock

Heat the oil in a large saucepan over moderate heat and add the onion. When tender, add the wine, mushrooms, thyme, bay leaf and the stock. Simmer for 15 minutes.

Involtini di vitello
Beef Rolls

Serves 4

600g (1¼ lb) tender beef
   (topside or steak)
4–5 large slices of Parma
   ham
sage leaves
50g (2 oz) butter

salt
freshly ground black
   pepper
3 tablespoons water
a knob of butter

Ask your butcher to slice the meat fairly thinly and in approximately 9cm (3½ inch) squares. You should get 2–3 pieces for each person. Flatten the slices on a board and on each one place half a slice of Parma ham. Add some large sage leaves, roll up and secure each with a toothpick. Melt the butter in a frying pan, add the rolls and season very little, because you must remember that the Parma ham is already salted. Cook very slowly on every side and when they are cooked through, add the water and a very small knob of butter. Bring it to a quick boil for 1 minute, stirring often, then remove the meat. Stir the gravy in the pan, add 2 more tablespoons of water, and return to the boil. Pour on top of the meat and serve at once.

Carne 'in umido'
Beef Casserole

Cooking *in umido* is when you cook in a casserole with a tomato sauce added. Literally, *umido* means damp or wet.

Carne

This refers to the liquid in the sauce, which will be of some consistency, but not too thick.

Often this type of cooking produces the whole meal, because the sauce will be used for the pasta course, then the meat will be eaten as the main course accompanied by some seasonal vegetables, or just some crusty bread which can mop up the remains of the *sugo* (juice). You can cook lots of things this way, including game, the cheapest cuts of any meat, fish, sausages and any leftovers.

Serves 4

600g (1¼ lb) stewing or braising steak
50g (2 oz) margarine
1 medium-sized onion, peeled and chopped
1 small carrot, thinly sliced
a few basil leaves
1 stick celery, chopped
salt
freshly ground black pepper
397g (14 oz) tin peeled tomatoes, chopped
1 tablespoon tomato purée
200g (7 fl oz) hot water

Remove excess fat from the meat, wash and cut it into large cubes, 4–5cm (2 inches) across. Melt the margarine in a flameproof casserole and cook the onion until tender. Add the carrot, the basil leaves and celery. Stir for a few seconds, then add the meat and season. Quickly brown the meat, turning it over often. Then add the tomatoes and the tomato purée diluted in 2 tablespoons of water. Stir and bring it to the boil. Now add the hot water, cover the pan and simmer for 1½–2 hours, stirring from time to time.

You can add potatoes to this dish. Peel 4 medium-sized potatoes, wash and thinly slice. Sprinkle with salt. Put them in the casserole over the meat, when the meat is nearly cooked (you should be able to push a fork through it easily). Add enough water to come to the same level as the potatoes, then simmer for a further 40 minutes.

Potacchio

Potacchio is a dish typical of The Marches, and of Ancona (its main town) in particular. You can use beef, lamb or chicken for this casserole – and even fish.

Serves 4

600g (1¼ lb) meat of your choice, trimmed and cubed
90ml (3 fl oz) olive oil
1 clove garlic (2 if you are very fond of it!), crushed
2 rosemary sprigs
salt

freshly ground black pepper
200ml (7 fl oz) wine, red or white
397g (14 oz) tin peeled tomatoes, chopped
1 tablespoon tomato purée
100ml (3½ fl oz) water

Put the meat in a large saucepan over moderate heat with the oil, garlic, rosemary, salt and pepper. Cook it until brown, stirring from time to time. Add the wine, then after 5 minutes, the strained tomatoes, and the purée diluted in 2 tablespoons of water. Simmer until tender, adding the rest of the water. It will need 1½–2 hours' cooking, depending on the meat you have used.

If you use fish, put all the other ingredients in first, then add the fish. The cooking time will be 30 minutes after you have added the fish. You do not need to add the remaining water.

San Lorenzo

Saint Lawrence night, on the tenth of August, is the night of the falling stars. When you see a *stella cadente*, make a wish and it will come true, so they say! It is one of the hottest nights of the year, during the *Solleone* (when the sun is in the sign of the lion), and an ideal night to have a barbecue in a field.

In my family this was a special day, and we always celebrated it with special food. We ended the day with an outdoor gathering where we ate *prosciutto*, melon, grilled steak, salad, water melon, all washed down with a good amount of local wine.

I have often been puzzled by the origin of this celebration of the barbecue in the open: maybe it is so that people could watch the spectacle of the falling stars while enjoying good food? Or maybe there was a more profound meaning to the occasion. After a lot of research and questioning, I have come up with one plausible suggestion: perhaps the traditional barbecue on that night originated from the type of horrendous death incurred by Saint Lawrence. He was in fact a martyr who encountered his end by being grilled over a great *graticola* (grating) on an open fire. *Graticola* is the long-handled grill used on open fires. The legend, or maybe history, says that he remained so impassive during his ordeal that he had the strength to look at his killers, saying, 'Turn me around, I am done on this side.'

San Lorenzo Day was a special day for me because my family owned a small church dedicated to him which dated back to AD 1100 – the oldest church in town. It used to be open only on that day, every year. On the days preceding this date, members of the family would have the task of cleaning the church, seeing that the bell rang, that the pictures and furniture were dusted, and water and wine put in the ampoules for the priest, together with a clean cloth for the altar.

The day would start with a Mass, then the church would remain open all day for any visitors and would be closed again at night after the evening service, to reopen only the following year. Our celebrations would then go on into the night, making it a memorable day, especially for the children. This was observed until war broke out, but then the church was sold, together with the land, and soldiers made a bonfire with its furniture.

Bistecche cotte alla brace
Barbecued Steak

Serves 4

4 tablespoons olive oil
1 garlic clove, crushed
juice of 1 lemon
500g (1¼ lb) beef steak

salt
freshly ground black pepper

Put the oil in a bowl, with the garlic and the lemon juice. Cut the steak, not too thickly, into portions, allowing two pieces per person, season with salt and pepper and put it in the marinade, turning the slices in the liquid. Leave them for at least 2 hours. Grill on both sides over the charcoal embers. Serve with a green salad and crusty bread.

Agnello lardellato
Pot-Roasted Lamb

First, I must say that Italian lambs are killed very young and a leg of lamb is very small and lean compared to lamb sold here.

Serves 4–5

fat from 6 slices of streaky bacon
1kg (2 lb) lamb, possibly the leg
salt
freshly ground black pepper
1 tablespoon fresh chopped parsley

1 spring onion, chopped
chopped fresh mixed herbs (marjoram, thyme, sage)
2 tablespoons fresh white breadcrumbs
1 teaspoon butter
200ml (7fl oz) wine

Cut the bacon fat into little cubes, make holes in the meat at regular intervals and push in the fat (as described on page 195). Rub the skin with salt, and add a little pepper. Mix the parsley, onion and mixed herbs with the breadcrumbs. Spread the butter on the bottom of an ovenproof dish, place the meat on top, and cover with the prepared mixture. Sprinkle a little salt and pour in the wine. Cover the dish and bake in a preheated oven for 1 hour at 180°C (360°F), gas mark 4. Test the meat with a skewer: if the juice is pink, leave it for another 20 minutes. Serve hot.

Testarelle arrosto
Roast Lambs' Heads

Serves 4

Roast heads are a real delicacy and you are lucky if you can get them from your butcher. They are sold split in half, and you will need one half per person.

Prick the eyes and squeeze them, or take them out with a pointed knife. Clean and wash the heads very well. Dry them, then rub a crushed clove of garlic all over the meat. Sprinkle with salt and chopped sage leaves. Remove the brains, soak them and peel off the membrane. Mop up the moisture, and put the brains back in place. Place the heads on a baking sheet, covering the brains with a piece of foil, and roast in a preheated oven at 180°C (360°F), gas mark 5, for about 30 minutes. Place under a hot grill, turning the heads over, until they are crisp all over.

Serve piping hot with a salad or crusty bread.

Cotolette alle cipolle Ⓕ
Sliced Beef with Onions

Serves 4

600g (1¼ lb) lean beef, topside, trimmed
salt
freshly ground black pepper
50g (2 oz) margarine

4 large onions, peeled and thinly sliced
100ml (3½ fl oz) olive oil
100ml (3½ fl oz) water
juice of 1 lemon

Cut the meat into fairly thin slices, flatten the pieces and season. Melt the margarine in a large frying pan and quickly fry the meat, turning once. Put the meat aside and keep hot. Fry the onions in the olive oil until tender, but not brown. Pour the liquid left over from frying the meat in an ovenproof dish, make a layer of onions, then a layer of the slices of meat and so on. Pour the water and the lemon juice over the top. Cover and cook in a preheated oven at 190°C (375°F), gas mark 5, for 45–60 minutes.

Fettine alla 'pizzaiola' Ⓕ
Sliced Beef 'Pizzaiola'

Serves 4

500g (1¼ lb) lean beef, topside, trimmed
100ml (3½ fl oz) olive oil
½ garlic clove, sliced
400g (1 lb) fresh pear-shaped tomatoes, skinned, seeded and sliced, or 397g (14 oz) tin peeled tomatoes

2 tablespoons fresh chopped parsley
100ml (3½ fl oz) white wine

Prepare the meat in slices as for the previous recipe, and quickly fry them in the oil. Slice the garlic in two or three pieces, so that you can remove it when the meat is cooked. In an ovenproof dish, arrange in layers some meat slices, then some pieces of tomatoes and parsley. When you have used up all these ingredients, pour the wine on the top and the juice collected in the frying pan. Cover the dish and bake in a preheated oven at 180°C (360°F), gas mark 4–5, for about 1 hour.

Cotoletta 'milanese'
'Milanese' Cutlets

Serves 4

600g (20 oz) veal cutlets,
  frying steak or chicken
  breasts, thinly sliced
salt
freshly ground black
  pepper

1 egg
fresh white breadcrumbs
oil for frying
lemon wedges for serving

See that the meat is very thinly sliced, then flatten it with a mallet. Sprinkle each cutlet with salt and pepper. Beat the egg and dip in the cutlets, then coat them with the breadcrumbs. Heat the oil in a frying pan and fry the cutlets until golden brown on both sides. As soon as you add the cutlets, lower the heat, so that they do not brown too quickly. When ready, lift them out on to a piece of white kitchen paper and keep them hot until you finish frying all the cutlets. Arrange them on a serving dish with wedges of lemon. Serve them with chips or with potato purée.

Cotoletta al formaggio [F]
Cheese Cutlets

Serves 4

500g (17 oz) veal cutlets,
  frying steak or chicken
  breasts
salt
freshly ground black
  pepper

1 egg
fresh white breadcrumbs
oil for frying
150g (6 oz) mozzarella
  cheese, thinly sliced, or
  any soft cheese

Cut the meat very thinly, as for *Cotoletta milanese* above. Proceed in the same way and fry the cutlets, then arrange them on a grill pan and place a slice of mozzarella cheese on each piece. Grill until the cheese melts. Serve at once.

If you want to prepare this dish in advance, you can freeze the cutlets as soon as they have cooled, but before adding the cheese. Put them in a foil dish. Make about 300ml (½ pint) tomato sauce by dissolving 1 tablespoon of tomato purée in 300ml (½ pint) water. Add a little salt, a teaspoon of margarine and boil for 15 minutes. Pour this sauce over the fried cutlets, cool, seal, label and freeze. The sauce will prevent the cutlets from drying up when frozen. To serve, remove from the freezer, put in a warm oven for 1 hour, then increase the heat and simmer for about 20 minutes. Remove the lid and make sure the cutlets are simmering. When ready and very hot, place on a grill pan, with a slice of cheese on top of each one and proceed to grill until the cheese melts.

Cotoletta alla parmigiana [Ⓕ]
Parmesan-Style Veal Cutlets

Serves 4

500g (17 oz) veal cutlets,
  beef steak or chicken
  breasts
salt
freshly ground black
  pepper
1 litre (1¾ pints) water
1 teaspoon margarine

50g (2 oz) tomato purée
1 egg
fresh white breadcrumbs
oil for frying
40g (1¼ oz) grated
  Parmesan cheese

Ask the butcher to thinly slice your meat. (If you are using chicken breasts, cut them into thin slices.) Flatten the slices with a mallet. Season. Put the water into a large saucepan with some salt and the margarine. Dissolve the tomato purée in a little extra water and add to the saucepan. Bring this to the boil and simmer for 30 minutes. Beat the egg and coat the meat in it, then press each slice on to the breadcrumbs so that both sides are covered. Heat the oil in a frying pan and quickly fry the meat until golden on both sides. Remove each cooked slice and drain on kitchen paper. Keep hot while cooking the remaining meat. Cover the bottom of a deep ovenproof dish with some of the sauce, then make a layer with the slices of meat, and sprinkle over some Parmesan cheese, followed by spoonfuls of the sauce, and continue until you have used up all the ingredients. There must be enough sauce just to cover the meat. Cover the dish and bake in a preheated oven at 180°C (360°F), gas mark 5, for 35–45 minutes.

Bistecche di maiale con finocchio Ⓕ
Pork Chops with Fennel

Serves 4

4 large pork ch.
salt
freshly ground black
  pepper
100ml (3 fl oz) Marsala or
  other fortified wine

½ garlic clove
a good pinch of dried fennel
  flowers or fennel seeds
1 tablespoon tomato purée
100ml (3 fl oz) red wine

Trim the chops and season with salt and pepper. Grill them slowly until cooked. When ready, lift them out of the pan on to a serving dish and keep them hot. Put the Marsala, garlic, fennel and tomato purée dissolved in the red wine into the pan and bring the mixture to the boil. Boil very quickly until the liquid has reduced to one-third of its original quantity. When this sauce is fairly thick, remove the garlic and pour over the chops. Serve at once.

Bistecche di maiale all'italiana
Italian-Style Pork Chops

Serves 4

4 large pork chops
salt
freshly ground black
* pepper*

a good pinch of rosemary
* leaves for each chop*
½ garlic clove, sliced

Sprinkle the chops with salt and pepper on both sides. Wash the rosemary leaves and spread them over each chop, with a couple of slices of garlic. Cover with foil and cook them in the oven at 220°C (425°F), gas mark 7, for 20 minutes. When they are nearly done, remove the foil, and brown them for 2–3 minutes under the grill. If the chops are not too thick you can cook them directly under the grill, turning them once or twice.

Polpettone
Meat Loaf

Serves 4

450g (1 lb) minced meat	salt
225g (8 oz) fresh white breadcrumbs	freshly ground black pepper
2 tablespoons fresh chopped parsley	50g (2 oz) grated Parmesan cheese
1 large carrot, diced	1 egg, lightly beaten
a pinch of cinnamon	2 tablespoons milk
a pinch of nutmeg	

In a basin, mix together the meat, breadcrumbs, parsley, carrot and spices, and season. When it is all well mixed together, add the Parmesan, then bind everything together with the egg and the milk. Shape this into a long thick sausage, rather like a small *salame*.

Take a clean cloth, a small napkin or a piece of clean muslin, and wrap your *polpettone* in it, twist the ends and tie them with some white cotton. Put it in a saucepan, cover with water, bring to the boil, and simmer for about 1¾ hours. When ready, lift it out of the liquid and leave it to cool. Remove the cloth and let the *polpettone* cool down completely. When cold, slice it and serve it cold with mayonnaise, accompanied by a green salad and sliced tomatoes.

Polpette
Meat Balls

In every household, no matter how careful you are in planning your meals, you will have leftovers at some point or another. *Polpette* are made with any leftover meat.

Serves 4–5

450g (1 lb) leftover meat
225g (8 oz) fresh white
  breadcrumbs
grated rind of ½ lemon
pinch of cinnamon
2 tablespoons grated
  Parmesan cheese

salt
freshly ground black
  pepper
1 egg, lightly beaten
2 tablespoons milk
flour for coating
oil for frying

Mince the meat together, even if it is of two different kinds. Put it in a large mixing bowl, add the breadcrumbs, lemon rind, cinnamon, Parmesan, salt and pepper. Mix everything well together and add the egg and milk to bind the mixture. Shape into small balls the size of a small egg, and roll each one in the palm of your hand. Roll them in some flour, then fry them in hot frying oil until brown on both sides. Use a fish slice to turn them, not a fork, or they might break. Drain them on some kitchen paper and serve piping hot.

You can serve them with a tomato sauce, which is, in fact, the most common way they are served in Italy. To make the sauce, melt a teaspoon of margarine in a saucepan and add salt, 300ml (½ pint) water and 2 tablespoons of tomato purée. Bring it to the boil, and simmer for about 15 minutes. Put the *polpette* in with the sauce and simmer for a further 15 minutes. Children will be encouraged to eat bread with this *sugo* or sauce.

Cotechino con lenticchie
Cotechino with Lentils

This dish is cooked in some parts of Italy in the New Year, but not necessarily on New Year's Day. Lentils are best eaten in the winter, as are all kinds of pulses, because you can buy the ones from the previous harvest. By the summer months they deteriorate and weevils can appear in them.

Serves 4

*a cotechino weighing
    about 450g (1 lb)*
2 onions
a stick of celery, chopped
275g (10 oz) lentils

100ml (3½ fl oz) olive oil
1 tablespoon tomato purée
*about 1.1 litres (2 pints)
    stock*

Put the *cotechino* in a deep saucepan, cover it with water, add one peeled and quartered onion and the celery. Bring to the boil, then let it simmer for about 2–2½ hours.

While the *cotechino* is cooking, prepare the lentils. Lentils are the only dry pulses which do not require soaking overnight before cooking. Make sure the lentils look healthy, without any black spots on them. Wash them well, then boil them in plenty of water until tender but not squashed. Drain and rinse in boiling water, then drain again. (They need rinsing because you will notice the water they have boiled in will be quite dark in colour.) When the *cotechino* is cooked, lift it out of the broth and keep hot. Chop the other onion and cook it until golden in the olive oil, then add the lentils and a little broth from the *cotechino*, stirring. Add the tomato purée diluted in 2 tablespoons of water, then, gradually, as much stock as necessary to simmer for about 25 minutes, stirring often. You may need to add a little water if it gets too thick.

Before you add any salt, taste the lentils, because the stock will be quite salty. If you should find that it is too salty, add a little water instead. To serve, cut the *cotechino* into slices, arrange on a serving dish and surround with the lentils. If you do not like lentils, you could serve *cotechino* with boiled rice. Flavour the rice, after cooking, with a few spoons of the stock.

Lumache
Snails

The snail festival takes place in Rome on St John's Day, 24 June. In other parts of Italy there is no special time for eating them, but everybody seems to agree that snails should not be picked after St Lawrence Day, 10 August. They say that maggots grow in the snails after that date and I do not think anybody wants to find that out for sure, so they stop eating them.

The night of 23 June is the night when you are supposed to be able to see witches on any crossroads at midnight. When the witches arrive, if you hold a broom upside down in your hands, they will not be able to touch you until they have counted all the bristles in the broom. By the time they finish this task, it will be dawn and they will have to retreat. The day before St John's Day, people in the countryside pick all sorts of wild flowers in great quantities, and mix them with walnut, oak, bay leaves and *santoreggia* (wild oregano). Yellow broom will abound among the flowers. They will put all these in a large tub full of water and leave it outside all night. The next morning they will have beautifully perfumed water to wash their faces with and to bath their babies. In some villages, in honour of the saint, the streets will be strewn with these flowers and leaves and as the people walk on them, the flowers will release their fragrance.

The snails that Romans eat are picked from the vineyards around Rome and they are of the best quality. Now snails are also imported from Albania. The wild ones are getting a little scarce so there are some farms where snails are raised for the food market.

I doubt if you can buy snails already cleaned and ready to cook. Even if they are supposed to be so, I would prefer to prepare them the way I know best. You start by leaving them in a covered pot (with some holes for air). Put a weight on the lid or the snails will find their way out. Many a time I got up in the morning to find the lid lifted up and snails sliding all over the kitchen walls! Leave the snails for about 4 days, 5 if they are very big ones, by which time they will have got rid of all they have eaten and they will be clean enough to eat. Wash them several times in cold water, then put them in a bowl with some vinegar and salt. They will make a lot of froth, and the remaining dirt will come out. Rinse them again well, then repeat the washing in a little vinegar (2–3 spoons, no more) and rinse until the water is really clean. There must be no sign of froth at all. Place the clean snails in a large saucepan covered in cold water. Put the saucepan on the stove and bring the heat on very, very gently. As the snails start coming out of their shells in the cold water, bring the water to the boil. The secret is to heat the water so gently that they do not realize any change in the temperature and do not go back completely in their shells before they get cooked. (I shall probably get some animal lover after me for this advice.) It will then be easier to eat them. Boil them for about 10 minutes, drain and rinse them. Leave them aside and prepare the sauce.

The snails I like best are the small ones, the size of a new penny, which grow in the cornfields on the stubble after the corn has been cut, or on long grass. During the month of July, early in the morning, you will see many people in Italy going out to pick this type of snails. The ones on the corn are the best because they take the taste of the plant they grow on, but you must be very careful not to pick any. from bushes that may have a bitter taste. You do not leave this type of snails for long before cooking them. One day is enough or they will die.

Wash and cook them in the same way as the big ones. These smaller snails are much cleaner and are great fun to eat. I do not suppose you get to pick your own snails but many people stay in farmhouses when they go on holiday, so you might just try for fun!

Serves 4

100ml (3½ fl oz) olive oil
2 spring onions or 1 medium-sized onion, chopped
6 very ripe pear-shaped tomatoes, skinned, seeded and chopped
1 tablespoon fresh chopped mint
2 tablespoons fresh chopped parsley
chopped leaves from 2 celery sticks
50g (2 oz) wild fennel, chopped
1 small pimento, chopped
1 clove garlic, crushed
salt
freshly ground black pepper
48 snails, cleaned

Heat the olive oil in a large frying pan and cook the onion until tender, then add the tomatoes, herbs and garlic and cook for about 5 minutes. Remove the garlic, then season the remaining mixture and add the snails. Simmer for 30 minutes, carefully stirring occasionally with a wooden spoon so that you don't break any shell. It is not advisable to swallow any bits or to crunch some with your teeth! Serve with the appropriate tool for getting the snails out of their shells; or you can always use a long pin.

Cervelli fritti
Fried Brains

This is regarded as a great delicacy in Italy, but it is a little difficult to obtain brains at times. You can get them from an abattoir or your butcher might be able to get you some.

Lambs' brains are usually used for frying, but you can also use veal.

Serves 4

100g (4 oz) lambs' brains per person (2 brains should be enough for 4 persons)
1 small onion, chopped
2 tablespoons chopped parsley
1 tablespoon vinegar
salt
1 tablespoon olive oil
juice of ½ lemon
plain flour
1 egg, beaten
oil for frying

Soak the brains in cold water, for about 10 minutes, to eliminate the blood, then put them in a saucepan, with the onion, half the parsley, the vinegar and some salt. Bring to the boil, lift out and put them in a basin of cold water. When they are cold, throw the water away and place on a clean cloth. Carefully remove all the membrane, then cut them into pieces. In another basin, mix these pieces with the olive oil, the lemon juice and the rest of the parsley. Leave them there for at least an hour, until you are ready to fry them. When the time comes, lift the pieces out, roll them in the flour and the egg and fry them in hot oil until golden all over. Serve them with slices of lemon.

Trippa
Tripe

Serves 4

25g (1 oz) lard
1 small onion, *peeled and
   chopped*
1 carrot, chopped
1 stick celery, chopped
350g (12 oz) fresh
   tomatoes

a pinch of marjoram
1.1kg (2 lb) tripe, sliced
salt
freshly ground black
   pepper

Heat the lard in a large frying pan and cook the onion, carrot and celery until tender. Add the tomatoes and cook for 15 minutes, then add the marjoram and tripe and cook for a further 15 minutes. Season, then simmer for 1 hour, adding a little water if necessary. Stir often.

7

Pollame e Cacciagione
Poultry and Game

Poultry

All types of poultry are popular in Italy, but a treat for a special occasion – like a wedding – is roast *faraona* (guinea fowl), which can be roasted like a pheasant and tastes a little dry but very delicate. As for chickens, an Italian housewife will use all parts of the bird, from the head to the feet and the entrails. When I went to a chicken farm in England I was shocked to see the farmer throwing away all those bits, but he probably would have been equally as horrified if I had said I could use them.

Pollo arrosto Ⓕ
Roast Chicken

Roasting a chicken is probably the easiest thing for
anybody to do and it might sound a little patronizing to tell
you how to do it. The reason for talking about it is that the
taste of your dish will very much depend on 'if' and how
you have prepared the bird. I say 'if', because I cannot
forget one Christmas a friend of mine was complaining that
her butcher had not given her the turkey giblets. On the
day, her husband proceeded to carry out the very British
task of carving at the table in front of family and guests,
and what do you think came out of the bird? The giblets,
still wrapped up in molten plastic! So, the first thing I do
when I buy a chicken is to take off all the string and start
from scratch.

Serves 4

1.75–2kg (4–4½ lb) chicken	juice of 1 lemon
salt	3 tablespoons olive oil
freshly ground black pepper	sage leaves
	rosemary leaves

Clean the chicken inside and out. Remove every feather
stump which may be left, then wash well by putting the
chicken in a large bowl filled with cold water and rub
inside and out with your hands. Lift it out and dry it with
kitchen paper. Put it back in the empty bowl and season
it with salt, inside and out. Rub some salt on the skin, and
a little pepper if you so wish.

Put the lemon juice and olive oil into a basin. Wash the
sage and rosemary leaves and spread them over the
chicken. Pour over the oil and lemon mixture, cover the

bowl and leave overnight. Next morning, lift the chicken out of the marinade, place it on a large piece of foil, pour the liquid over it and close the foil around the bird.

Bake it in a preheated oven at 190°C (375°F), gas mark 5, for about 1 hour, then open the foil, baste it and with a long needle see if the juice that comes out of the thick part of the thigh is still pink. If it is, leave the chicken for 20 minutes longer, before removing the foil. When the foil is removed, test again with a fork. Increase the temperature to 220°C (425°F), gas mark 7, and bake the chicken, without the foil, for a further 20 minutes turning it over and basting it, so that the skin will crisp up all over.

You can freeze a roast chicken very successfully. It saves a lot of time and nobody knows the difference! After the chicken has cooked in foil for 1 hour, take out of the oven and leave it to cool down, still in the foil. When it is completely cold, pop the foil-wrapped chicken into a cellophane bag, seal, label and freeze. To defrost, remove from the freezer the night before, then in the morning take off the foil, place the chicken in a greased baking dish, pour the liquid on the top, cover the breast with 4 slices of unsmoked streaky bacon. Cook it for about 25 minutes, in a preheated oven, at 180°C (350°F), gas mark 4, basting it a few times, then test it with a needle. If ready, increase the heat to 220°C (425°F), gas mark 7, and cook for another 20 minutes, removing the bacon and turning it around on the back and sides so that it will be crisp all over.

Pollo alla cacciatora Ⓕ
Chicken the Hunter's Way

Serves 4–5

1.5kg (3 lb) chicken
½ clove garlic, crushed

200ml (7 fl oz) white wine
397g (14 oz) tin tomatoes

For the marinade
salt
freshly ground black
  pepper
sage and rosemary leaves

juice of 1 lemon
200ml (7 fl oz) olive oil

Clean and wash the chicken inside and out. Cut it into pieces. Cut the drumsticks in two and continue cutting pieces of about the same size. Place all the pieces in a large bowl, sprinkle with salt and pepper, and add a good amount of washed rosemary and sage leaves. Pour the lemon juice, mixed with one third of the olive oil, on top of the chicken. Cover the bowl and leave for at least 6 hours or overnight.

Heat the remaining oil in a very large frying pan, and brown the chicken pieces with the garlic. Turn the meat often and when they are brown on both sides, remove the garlic and add the wine. After about 5 minutes, add the liquid from the marinade, with all the herbs. Stir occasionally, for a further 5 minutes, then strain in the tomatoes from the tin.

Place all the ingredients in an ovenproof dish, cover and cook in a preheated oven at 190°C (375°F), gas mark 5, for about 1½ hours.

You could finish cooking the chicken in the frying pan, but if you do you must stir often, to make sure it does not stick. I prefer to put it in the oven and forget about it. You can freeze this dish very successfully.

Tacchino allo spiedo
Turkey Kebabs

Buy a small, compact, juicy bird – a hen is best. Clean the turkey, pulling out all the feather stubble left in it. Wash it inside and out. Wipe it dry with a towel.

Serves 8

4kg (9 lb) turkey
a sprig of rosemary
350g (12 oz) streaky
   unsmoked rindless bacon

sage leaves

For the marinade
juice of 2 lemons
2 tablespoons olive oil

a good quantity of large
sage leaves for roasting

Prepare the marinade by squeezing the lemons and mixing the juice with the oil. Wash the sage and rosemary. Cut the turkey into small pieces, about 4–5cm (1½–2 inches) across. As you do this, try to remove as many of the bones as you can. Place all the pieces in a large bowl and pour over the marinade. Cover and leave overnight.

Wash the large sage leaves and cut up the bacon into squares of roughly the same size as the turkey cubes. If you have a proper spit, all is well; if not, use small barbecue skewers. On the spit, alternate a piece of bacon with a sage leaf and a piece of turkey, and so on. Do not push the pieces tightly; they should only just touch. If you are using small skewers, place them next to one another on a roasting tin with the ends resting on the sides. There must be a gap between the meat and the bottom of the tin.

Cook in a preheated oven at 200°C (400°F), gas mark 6, for about 40 minutes, but for an extra 10 minutes at a higher temperature if you like the meat very crisp. While cooking, baste the meat first with the marinade, then with the juice that collects at the bottom of the tin. When cooked, push the meat off the skewers and arrange the pieces on a serving dish. Make a green salad to accompany this roast. Rub the salad bowl with a small clove of garlic and add some fennel to the salad.

Tacchino arrosto con ripieno di castagne
Roast Turkey with Chestnut Stuffing

Prepare the turkey as you would for the previous recipe, but do not cut it into pieces. Marinate it in the same way.

Serves 8

4kg (9 lb) turkey
6 slices of streaky bacon for
the breast

For the stuffing
20 chestnuts
20 green olives, stoned and chopped
6 sausages, skinned

1 egg, lightly beaten
a few pieces of black truffle (optional)

Prepare the stuffing first. Boil the chestnuts until tender and peel them before they get cold. Mash them with a fork. In a large basin, mix the chestnut purée, olives, truffle and sausages to form a paste, adding the egg to bind the ingredients together. Fill the neck of the turkey, pushing the stuffing carefully so you do not leave any air bubbles. Pull the skin to cover the opening and sew it with a needle and white cotton. If you have any mixture left, push it in the other end of the turkey.

Cover the breast with the bacon, keeping it in place with some cotton. Wrap the turkey in foil and cook in a preheated oven at 180°C (350°F), gas mark 4, for about 2–2½ hours. After this amount of cooking time, take the foil off, bake for another 20 minutes, then remove the bacon from the breast. Increase the temperature to 220°C (475°F), gas mark 7, baste and turn the turkey around, so the skin will be crisp, and roast for a further 20–30 minutes.

Cappone arrosto farcito
Roasted Stuffed Capon

Serves 6–8

3kg (7 lb) capon
salt
4 slices streaky bacon

lemon slices, to decorate

For the stuffing
2 tablespoons packet sage and onion stuffing
1 capon liver or chicken liver
2 tablespoons fresh white breadcrumbs

1 tablespoon grated Parmesan cheese
a pinch of cinnamon
a pinch of nutmeg
1 egg, lightly beaten

For the marinade
juice of 1 lemon
100ml (3½ fl oz) olive oil
sage leaves

a sprig of rosemary
1 clove of garlic, crushed

Clean and wash the capon. Mix the lemon juice and oil together with the washed sage leaves, rosemary and garlic.

Sprinkle the inside of the capon with salt, rub some on the skin, and place it in a large bowl, pour the marinade over. Cover and leave overnight.

Prepare the stuffing. Mix the sage and onion stuffing with enough boiling water to make a smooth paste. Leave it to cool. Clean and wash the liver and chop up. In a large basin, mix the liver with the breadcrumbs, sage and onion stuffing, cheese, cinnamon and nutmeg. Make it into a smooth paste, using the egg to bind it together.

Lift the capon out of the marinade, stuff its neck with this mixture. Sew it up with white cotton. If there is any stuffing left over, push it in the inside of the bird. Place the capon in a greased roasting tin, and pour the marinade over. Cover the breast with the bacon. Roast for about 2 hours in a preheated oven at 180°C (350°F), gas mark 4, basting from time to time with the juice from the bottom of the dish. When you can easily push a fork into the flesh and the juice that comes out is clear, remove the bacon. Increase the heat to 230°C (450°F), gas mark 8, and turn the capon a couple of times, so that the skin will get crisp all over. It will need about 15 minutes at a higher temperature. Carve it, and decorate with lemon slices.

Uccelli allo spiedo
Birds on the Spit

You can use any small bird, and you need a good number of sage leaves, unsmoked streaky bacon (1 slice per bird), salt and freshly ground black pepper.

Clean, wash and dry the birds. Arrange them on kebab skewers with alternate sage leaves and slices of bacon. Baste while cooking with a little lard.

Polenta con uccelli
Polenta with Birds

For this dish you can use quail and other small birds.

Serves 4

2–3 *birds per person*
3 *slices streaky unsmoked*
  bacon
2 *tablespoons olive oil*

1 *stick celery, chopped*
1 *carrot, chopped*
2 *397g (14 oz) tins peeled*
  tomatoes

For the marinade
lemon juice
1 *small glass brandy*
1 *onion, peeled and*
  chopped

salt
freshly ground black
  pepper

Clean and wash the birds. Marinate them overnight in a mixture of the lemon juice, brandy and onion, seasoned with salt and pepper.

Fry the bacon in the oil, add the celery and carrot and the marinated birds with the liquid from the marinade. Stir and cook until tender, adding a little stock. When you easily spike a fork through them, add the tomatoes, mix well and cook a further 30 minutes. Keep this hot while you make polenta (see page 169).

Use the *sugo* (juice) to spread on polenta and place the birds on top.

Piccioni farciti arrosto
Roasted Stuffed Pigeons

I am not going to tell you to cook the pigeons you see in your garden! Pigeons for roasting are raised for the table and you can buy them in the best food shops. They must be young and tender birds.

Serves 4

2 pigeons

For the marinade
salt
freshly ground black
  pepper

a pinch of nutmeg
100ml (3½ fl oz) white
  wine

For the stuffing
2 chicken livers
4 slices streaky bacon
100g (4 oz) beef steak
50g (2 oz) butter or
  margarine
1 onion, peeled and
  chopped

a pinch of nutmeg
a pinch of cinnamon
a pinch of dried thyme
1 bay leaf, chopped
1 egg, lightly beaten

You need half a pigeon per person. Clean and wash the pigeons inside and out. Dry them. Sprinkle with some salt, pepper and a small pinch of nutmeg. Place them in a glass dish and pour the white wine on them. Cover them and leave to marinate overnight.

Prepare the stuffing. Clean and slice the chicken livers. Cut the bacon into strips, discarding the rind. Chop the steak. Melt 1 teaspoon butter or margarine in a large frying pan and slowly fry the onion and bacon. When the onion is tender, add the steak, increasing the heat and stirring, then add the liver. Season with salt, pepper, nutmeg, cinnamon, thyme and the bay leaf. Stir and cook very quickly for 1 minute.

Now strain the liquid from this mixture, leave it aside in reserve, then mince all the strained pieces. If you do not have a mincer, you could chop them up very finely. When minced, add the egg and a teaspoon of butter or margarine, mix well and set aside.

Lift the pigeons out of the marinade, divide the stuffing and stuff the necks of each bird. Take some white cotton and a needle and sew up the opening. If you have any stuffing left over, place it in the bird's body.

Place the stuffed pigeons in an ovenproof dish, with the remaining butter, melted. Mix ½ glass of water with the reserved marinade and pour a little over the pigeons (about 2 tablespoons on each). Cook the pigeons for about 30 minutes in a preheated oven at 180°C (350°F), gas mark 4, then pour the rest of the marinade over them, turn them around and cook for a further 30 minutes. Remove the white cotton before serving. Quarter the pigeons, and serve them with a mixed salad.

Anitra farcita arrosto
Stuffed Roast Duck
Serves 4

2–2.5kg (5–6 lb) duck
salt
freshly ground black
  pepper

6 slices streaky unsmoked
  bacon

For the marinade

1 small onion, peeled and
  chopped
2 tablespoons olive oil
4 tablespoons red wine

juice of ½ lemon
3 sage sprigs
a pinch of oregano

For the stuffing

duck gizzard, heart and
  liver
4 sage leaves
2 slices onion
4 tablespoons fresh white
  breadcrumbs

2 tablespoons grated
  Parmesan cheese
⅓ teaspoon cinnamon
a pinch of oregano
1 egg, lightly beaten

For the gravy

300ml (½ pint) water	½ chicken stock cube
1 tablespoon flour mixed with 2 tablespoons water	juice of 1 orange

Clean the duck and pull out all the feather stubble. If you have a gas oven, burn them off on top of a small flame, then pull out the thicker ones. Thoroughly wash the duck inside and out, dry with a paper towel and then season, in and out, with salt and pepper. Cover the breast with the bacon. Put the duck in a large dish with a lid. Mix together all the marinade ingredients and pour over the duck. Leave it for 5–6 hours or overnight, basting several times. Cover.

To prepare the stuffing, clean the gizzard, pull out the inner skin and wash well, then cut off the tough inside part and chop the rest. Wash the heart, getting rid of all the blood, and chop. Put the heart and gizzard in a food processor for a few moments, take it out and get rid of the pieces of hard skin which will now come away easily. Wash the liver and make sure the whole gall bag has been removed, or there will be green patches which you must cut off. Beat together the liver, sage and onion, adding the shredded gizzard and heart to form a paste. Put them in a basin, add the breadcrumbs, Parmesan cheese, salt, pepper, cinnamon and oregano. Mix well, then bind this stuffing with the egg. Remove the duck from the marinade, and fill the neck cavity with the stuffing, sewing the opening with white cotton. If there is any stuffing left, put it inside the body, together with a few washed sage leaves. Grease an ovenproof dish, place the duck on it and cover the breast with the bacon. Pour the marinade over and roast it in a preheated oven at 180°C (360°F), gas mark 4, for 1 hour 15 minutes, basting from time to time. With a carving fork, prod the thickest part to see if the duck is tender, otherwise cook it for a little longer, say another 15 minutes. Remove the bacon, prick the skin with a fork, then put the duck back in the oven for a further 20 minutes at 200°C (400°F), gas mark 6, turning it and basting. By this time the skin should be really crisp and brown all over. Lift the duck on to a serving dish if you want to take it whole to the table, otherwise put it on a board and carve. Whether or not you carve it, cover the duck with foil and keep it hot while you make a gravy to serve with it.

To make the gravy, pour away all the fat from the tin, just leaving a little liquid at the bottom. Add the water and stir with a wooden spoon, so all the goodness left will mix with the water. Pour the smooth flour paste into the tin, together with the crumbled chicken cube, orange juice, salt and pepper. Mix and boil it for 1 minute, then strain and pour it into a gravy jug.

Sugo con anitra
Duck Sauce

This sauce is ideal for polenta (page 169) and pasta dishes (page 144).

Serves 5–6

2–3kg (5–6 lb) duck
1 medium-sized onion,
   peeled and chopped
duck liver, chopped
handful each of basil,
   marjoram and oregano
   leaves

2 397g (14 oz) tins Italian
   peeled tomatoes
1 tablespoon tomato purée
400ml (14 fl oz) water
salt
freshly ground black
   pepper

Pollame e Cacciagione

For the marinade

1 celery stick	juice of ½ lemon
1 carrot	3 sprigs sage
1 small onion, chopped	1 pinch oregano
2 tablespoons olive oil	

Clean the duck. Mix together the marinade, pour it over the duck, and leave overnight. When it has marinated, cut it into 10–12 pieces and put it aside. Slowly cook the chopped onion in the marinade until tender. Now add the chopped liver and herbs, and the duck pieces. Over a low heat, let the duck cook, so that its fat melts, for about 40 minutes, stirring occasionally. Add the strained tomatoes and the tomato purée diluted in half the water. Season. Simmer for a further 45 minutes until the meat is well cooked and the sauce fairly thick. If the duck is still hard when you push a fork in, add the rest of the water and cook for a little longer.

Use this sauce on top of polenta or for a pasta dish. Place some of the pieces of meat on top of each portion. You can also cook a young goose this way.

Game

While France has always been a country of fishermen, Italy has always been a country of *cacciatori*, which literally means hunters, with a shotgun. Towards the end of August every year, one day is sacred to nearly all men, young and old, who can (and even cannot) use a shotgun. In fact it would be better to say 'who have the use of' a shotgun. This day is the start of the shooting season. No work or family commitments will be honoured, and every available male will be up at the crack of dawn, ready to walk miles, even for the sake of sometimes coming back with only a few birds in his bag.

And beware of wishing a *cacciatore* good luck. It is unlucky. The only accepted wish is '*In bocca al lupo*' ('In the wolf's mouth'), to which the answer is '*Crepi il lupo*' ('Burst the wolf'). After this rigmarole, he can happily start on his trek.

Things have changed in recent years as many parts of the country have been made *riserva di caccia*, where shooting is forbidden, to give the animals a chance, and birds raised in captivity are set free. Even so, the stock has been devastated. One of the reasons is that birds raised by man do not acquire the experience and knowledge of defence which wild birds have, so the foxes are multiplying at their expense.

There used to be eagles on our mountains, but gradually the bigger species have disappeared and even the smaller ones have now been decimated. Wild boar are coming back in the woods – as is the wolf, which is now protected. At one time Italians would shoot anything that flew, except swallows, as there was, and I think still is, a law against killing them. I have heard Australians complaining that their birds were disappearing after the Italians started to emigrate to their country. Now, shooting is allowed only about two days each week in the season and many hunters are giving up this sport because of the many restrictions that are imposed every year. Probably because of the old hunting traditions, game plays a great part in Italian cooking. All game must be well hung. Do not think I am trying to put you off when I repeat a hunter's saying: 'Game is good when it starts to smell.'

Coniglio fritto
Fried Rabbit

Rabbit has always been a very acceptable and appreciated item on an Italian menu. Perhaps, now that beef has become so expensive, it will be worthy of some consideration also in other countries. I am talking about rabbits especially raised for the table, not the wild ones which could be very tough and have a flavour of wild game.

Serves 4–5

1 rabbit	fresh white breadcrumbs
salt	oil for frying
freshly ground black pepper	lemon slices for serving
1 egg, lightly beaten	

For the marinade
100ml (3½ fl oz) olive oil   sage leaves and rosemary
juice of 1 lemon   oregano

Clean and wash the rabbit thoroughly. Cut it into pieces (3 from each leg), slice the body crossways, making sure the slices are not thicker than about 1cm (½ inch). Prepare a marinade with the olive oil, lemon juice, washed sage leaves and rosemary and a pinch of oregano. Sprinkle the meat with salt and pepper, place it in a deep dish and pour the marinade over it. Cover and leave for about 6 hours or overnight.

Lift the pieces out of the marinade and coat the meat with the egg, then roll each piece in a bowl of breadcrumbs, making sure it is coated all over. Heat some oil in a large frying pan and gently fry the rabbit pieces until golden. Turn the pieces over a couple of times and fry at medium heat to make sure the meat is well cooked and not just brown on the surface. Serve with slices of lemon.

Coniglio arrosto
Roast Rabbit

Prepare the rabbit by cleaning and washing it. Do not cut it. Sprinkle salt all over, rub the outside skin with a crushed clove of garlic and proceed to marinate it as explained in the previous recipe. Lift it out of the marinade, place a washed sprig of rosemary and a few sage leaves inside. Place the rabbit on a piece of foil, pour the liquid from the marinade over it and close the foil. Cook for 1½–2 hours in a preheated oven at 180°C (350°F), gas mark 4. Test if it is tender with the prongs of a long fork. Take the foil off, baste it with the liquid and give it 15–20 more minutes at 200°C (400°F), gas mark 6, turning it once or twice so that the meat can crispen all over.

It is nice to roast some potatoes together with the rabbit. Wash the leaves from two sprigs of rosemary. Peel and cut 4 large potatoes in quarters, sprinkle them with salt and a little olive oil. Mix the rosemary with them and arrange them around the rabbit, if there is room in the same tin. If not, place them in another greased baking tray. They will take about 1 hour to cook. Rosemary gives an extra special flavour to potatoes.

Coniglio in porchetta
Porchetta of Rabbit

Porchetta is a way of cooking pork, as the word suggests, but it is a very tasty way of cooking other meats, including rabbit.

Serves 6

1 rabbit
salt
rosemary
2 tablespoons chopped wild
   fennel leaves
rabbit liver and heart
225g (8 oz) minced beef

4 slices rindless unsmoked
   bacon
freshly ground black
   pepper
3 eggs, lightly beaten
some knobs of lard

Clean and wash the rabbit well. Dry, and rub the outside and inside with salt. Wash a good quantity of rosemary and sprinkle over the outside. Mix the fennel with the liver and heart and minced beef.

In a large frying pan, fry the bacon, add the beef mixture, season with salt and pepper and bind this mixture with the eggs. Remove from the heat. Fill the inside of the rabbit with this stuffing and sew it up with strong white cotton. Place the rabbit on a piece of foil, dotted with little knobs of lard. Close the foil and place it in an ovenproof dish. Cook it in a preheated oven at 180°C (350°F), gas mark 4, for about 1½ hours. Test if the meat is tender with the prongs of a long fork, and when it is, open the foil and cook for another 15–20 minutes, at 200°C (400°F), gas mark 6, to brown it all over. Turn once or twice.

Pappardelle con lepre
Pappardelle with Hare

Pappardelle are a type of pasta, larger than tagliatelle, and nearer the width of lasagne.

Serves 6

1 hare
25g (1 oz) butter
4 slices rindless unsmoked streaky bacon, chopped
1 medium-sized onion, peeled and chopped
1 stick of celery, chopped
salt
freshly ground black pepper
pinch of thyme
1 tablespoon flour

1 glass white wine
2 tablespoons tomato purée
500ml (18 fl oz) stock or stock cube dissolved in water
homemade pasta made with 6 eggs (see page 144)
about 750g (1 lb 10 oz) plain flour
grated Parmesan cheese

Some people cut up the hare, taking all the bones out; others just cut the hare in pieces and serve it with the bones. It is obviously much quicker to do the latter and it does not alter the taste of the dish. So, clean and wash the hare and cut it into small pieces. Melt the butter in a large frying pan and cook the bacon and onion and celery. When the onion is tender, add the meat, seasoning with salt and pepper and a pinch of thyme. Sir often, adding the flour when the meat is getting brown all over. Stir in the wine and 10 minutes later dilute the tomato purée in some of the stock. Add this to the meat, then add the remaining stock. Cover the saucepan and simmer until the hare is cooked, about 1½ hours. The *sugo* (gravy) should by then be rather thick. If it is too thin, let it boil uncovered for a short time.

Make the pasta while the sauce cooks. When the sauce

is ready, boil it and serve it with grated Parmesan, the sauce from the hare and, on top of each plate, a few pieces of the meat.

Lepre al tegame
Hare Casserole

Serves 4–5

1 hare
4–5 tablespoons olive oil
40g (1½ oz) butter
1 onion
1 garlic clove
1 stick of celery
50g (2 oz) ham

salt
freshly ground black
  pepper
200ml (7 fl oz) white wine
1 tablespoon tomato purée
200ml (7 fl oz) water

Clean the hare, cut it into pieces, wash and dry the pieces. Melt the olive oil and butter in a large frying pan and fry the onion, garlic, celery and ham for a few minutes, then add the hare and cook slowly until brown. Season it. Add a little of the wine at intervals, stirring often. When all the wine is absorbed remove the garlic and add the tomato purée diluted in the water and simmer until tender.

Lepre arrosto
Roast Hare

Serves 4–5

1 hare
2 garlic cloves
2 sprigs of rosemary, finely
  chopped
4 juniper berries

juice of 1 lemon
salt
200ml (7 fl oz) olive oil
25g (1 oz) butter

Clean the hare. Finely cut the cloves of garlic and the rosemary, and mix with the juniper and the lemon juice. Spread this all over the hare together with salt. Also sprinkle salt inside the hare. Leave it for two days, covered, in the refrigerator. Place in a large saucepan over moderate heat with the oil and butter and cover. Stir often while it cooks, adding a little water now and then. When it is cooked (test it with a long fork or a skewer), increase the heat so it will be golden brown all over.

Beccaccia al tegame
Woodcock Casserole

You can also cook pheasant this way.

Serves 2

1 woodcock
salt
freshly ground black
   pepper
a little thyme and
   marjoram, chopped
25g (1 oz) lard
1 tablespoon olive oil
1 bay leaf, chopped

2 tablespoons cognac
100ml (3½ fl oz) stock
1 small onion, chopped
4 chicken livers, chopped
1 teaspoon butter
100ml (3½ fl oz) white
   wine
1 tablespoon flour

Clean the bird inside and out, and mop up any surplus moisture. Sprinkle inside and out with salt and pepper, thyme and marjoram. Fry the lard, oil and bay leaf in a frying pan for 1 minute, then add the woodcock to the pan. Cook it until brown all over, turning often. Pour in the cognac, cover with a lid, and simmer using a little of the stock, until the meat is well cooked. Now lift out the bird and cut it in half lengthwise. Keep it warm. Fry the onion and livers in a pan with the butter, season and add the wine. Mix the flour with the remaining stock and add to the pan when the wine has evaporated. Add it gradually, stirring all the time. Cook for 15 minutes, then strain everything and pour the livers and sauce over the bird, discarding the fat. Serve at once.

8

Dolci
Desserts

Italians on the whole are not great pudding or cake eaters, but they make an exception at Christmas and Easter when *panettone* and *colomba* are consumed in great quantities. Nevertheless, there is a great variety of dessert dishes typical of Italy and I have given a few of my favourite recipes here. A strange Italian habit, for instance, is to eat buns, doughnuts or other sweet things at breakfast time. This mostly concerns men going to work. They will leave the house after drinking an espresso coffee, go to the office or their place of work, then, after about 1–2 hours, they will have a walk to the nearest café to have a cappuccino or another espresso and they will eat any bun or pastry they fancy. Some may do that on their way to work, if they cannot get out later on.

Dolci

Very little milk is used for breakfast in Italian households, unless there are small children. Puddings are reserved mostly for Sundays and for anniversaries and other celebrations. Fresh fruit always appears on Italian tables to be eaten at the end of every meal. If a pudding is served, fruit will be eaten afterwards. No fruit at the end of a meal means a very poor household, and a great punishment for a child in disgrace is to be sent to bed without fruit. A favourite Italian dessert is cheese eaten with pears.

Nove Maggio Ⓕ
Ninth of May

I call this sweet 'Ninth of May' because I invariably make it for that day, not to celebrate the end of the last war, but a family anniversary.

Serves 10

1 packet gelatine powder
4 tablespoons cold water
50g (2 oz) bitter chocolate
5 egg yolks
150g (6 oz) sugar
3 egg whites

4 tablespoons Amaretto liqueur
250g (10 oz) ricotta, crumbled
275ml (½ pint) double cream

Dissolve the gelatine in the cold water in a basin. Break up the chocolate into small pieces and add it to the gelatine. Place the basin in a bowl containing boiling water, so it will dissolve, stirring from time to time.

In the meantime, whisk the yolks and the sugar until fluffy. Beat the whites in a separate basin until stiff peaks form. Add the liqueur to the egg yolks and beat well.

Then stir in the gelatine. Go on whisking, until well mixed, then fold in the egg whites. Mix the ricotta with the double cream, giving it a vigorous stir with a wooden spoon. Then add to the other ingredients folding it in with a spatula.

Dampen a 1½ litre (3 pint) basin and pour in the mixture. Cover with foil and place in the refrigerator for at least 2 hours before serving. To serve this sweet, turn it out on to a serving dish, decorating it with a little whipped cream, or cherries, or grated chocolate.

You can freeze this sweet. Sometimes I make two with this amount, dividing it into two basins. I then use one and freeze the other.

Fragole
Strawberries

If you prepare the strawberries this way you can avoid eating cream. Hull the strawberries, wash them and cut them in half. Mountain strawberries should be left whole. Sprinkle some caster sugar on them and the juice of one lemon for each 400g (1 lb) of fruit. Mix well and put in the fridge, covered, for at least 2 hours before serving. An alternative to lemon juice is a glass of white wine.

Budino di fragole Ⓕ
Strawberry Mousse

This is a good sweet to make if you have a glut of strawberries or if they are getting too ripe and need to be used up. It can also be made with blackberries, raspberries or blackcurrants.

Serves 4–6

450g (1 lb) strawberries,
  hulled
75g (3 oz) caster sugar
juice of ½ lemon
1 packet of gelatine
2 egg whites

150ml (¼ pint) double
  cream
whole strawberries for
  decoration
whipped cream for
  decoration

Place the strawberries in a food processor with the sugar, and blend for a few moments. Add the lemon juice and mix well. Dissolve the gelatine in a basin, with 2 tablespoons cold water, then add the same amount of boiling water and stir until the gelatine is dissolved. Stand the basin in hot water for a little while, stirring until the gelatine is clear. Leave it to cool, then add it to the strawberries. Beat the egg whites until stiff, then fold them a little at a time into the cold mixture with a spatula. Whip the cream. When thick, but still of a running consistency, carefully fold into the strawberry mixture. Pour the mixture into a clean, damp basin or any deep dish and put it in the refrigerator for a few hours. To serve it, turn out on to a serving dish and decorate with a few fresh strawberries or just some whipped cream.

If you freeze this mousse, remove from the freezer about 2–3 hours before serving. You can also use frozen strawberry purée. Blend the strawberries into a purée, adding 75g (3 oz) of sugar for each 450g (1 lb) of fruit, then freeze.

Zabaglione with Amaretto Ⓕ

Marsala is the dessert wine from Marsala, in Sicily, and Amaretto is a liqueur made with almonds. You could use some medium sherry as an alternative together with a teaspoon of almond essence.

Serves 6

4 egg yolks
4 tablespoons caster sugar
4 tablespoons Marsala and
  1 tablespoon Amaretto
1 packet of gelatine
4 egg whites

150ml (¼ pint) double
  cream
4 sponge cakes, sprinkled
  with Amaretto
whipped cream for
  decoration

Mix together the egg yolks, the sugar and the Marsala in a large basin. Stand the basin over a saucepan of simmering water and beat the mixture with a hand whisk until it is fluffy and creamy. It will increase in volume very considerably, so you need a very large basin. Continue to whisk while the mixture thickens, then remove the basin from the heat. Melt the gelatine in 2 tablespoons cold water, add 2 tablespoons boiling water and mix well. Pour the gelatine into the mixture, whisk well and keep beating until cool. Leave it to get cold, but not set, while you beat the egg whites to peaks. With a spatula, fold these in, then whip the cream to thick but still pouring consistency, and fold in.

Pour everything into a damp basin. It must not come higher than at least 2.5cm (1 inch) from the top. Slice 4 sponge trifle cakes and place them on top, when the mixture is starting to set. Cover the basin with a lid or a plate and put it in the refrigerator. Leave it for at least 3–4 hours or overnight. To serve, turn it out on to a serving dish (the sponge cakes will be at the bottom now). Decorate with whipped cream.

You can serve zabaglione in individual portions, in crystal cups. In this case, line the glass containers with some sponge cake, sprinkle with Amaretto and pour some of the zabaglione on top. When set, decorate with whipped cream.

Zuppa inglese
English Soup

Serves 6

3 eggs and 1 extra yolk
4 tablespoons sugar
2 tablespoons cornflour
900ml (1½ pints) milk
a strip of lemon rind
a small piece of cinnamon
   stick
1 tablespoon cocoa mixed
   with 1 tablespoon caster
   sugar

6 trifle sponge cakes or 12
   sponge fingers
3 tablespoons Marsala and
   2 tablespoons Amaretto
   or just over 3 tablespoons
   Alchermes

Beat the eggs and the extra yolk with the sugar. In a basin dissolve the cornflour in 2–3 tablespoons of the milk, then mix it with the eggs and, while mixing, gradually add the remaining milk, lemon rind and cinnamon stick. Place in a saucepan over moderate heat and mix continuously while it gradually comes to the boil and thickens. It should only just boil, before you remove it from the heat. Discard the lemon and cinnamon. Pour half of the custard into a basin and gradually add to it the cocoa and sugar mixed together. Blend well, making sure there are no lumps. Line the bottom of an oval serving dish with the sponge cakes. If you are using the trifle sponge cakes, cut them in half. With a spoon, sprinkle the Marsala and Amaretto on the cakes. Pour some of the yellow custard over them, then some of the mixture with the chocolate. Alternate the two until they are both used up. Refrigerate and serve when cool.

Zuppa romana
Roman Soup

Serves 4

2 tablespoons flour
500ml (18 fl oz) milk
2 eggs, lightly beaten
2 tablespoons sugar
a piece of lemon rind
a stick of cinnamon

6 tablespoons jam
16 sponge fingers
some Alchermes or
 Curaçao
150ml (¼ pint) double
 cream

Make a custard by dissolving the flour with some of the milk. Add the eggs, the sugar, lemon rind and cinnamon stick, then pour in the remaining milk. Place in a saucepan over low heat, stirring continuously until it thickens and comes to the boil. Boil for only 1 minute, then remove from the heat and discard the lemon rind and cinnamon stick. Spread half the jam on the bottom of a greased ovenproof dish, then make a layer of sponge fingers sprinkled with Alchermes or Curaçao, followed by a layer of the custard and half of the cream. Make another layer with 3 tablespoons of jam, the rest of the sponge fingers, custard and cream. Keep in refrigerator before serving for at least 2 hours.

Torta di gelato [E]
Ice Cream Cake

This is a variation of the Marsala cake. You will need the same ingredients as for Marsala cake (see page 267) and 1–2 family blocks of vanilla ice cream.

Serves 12

Prepare everything as for the Marsala cake. When you have made the first layer of sponge cakes, spread some mixture on it, then take the block of ice cream, cut it quickly horizontally and make a layer of ice cream. Work fast, or the ice cream will melt in the process. You can make another layer of ice cream if you wish, over the next layer of mixture, but in this case you will need a deeper dish.

As soon as you put the weight on top, put the cake into the freezer. Leave the weight for a couple of hours, then the cake is ready to serve. This cake freezes very successfully.

Gelato a sorpresa ©Ⓕ
Ice Cream Surprise

Serves 6

4 eggs, separated
4 tablespoons caster sugar
2 tablespoons cocoa
150ml (¼ pint) double
  cream

1 block vanilla ice cream,
  family size

Beat the egg yolks with the sugar, until very creamy and fluffy. Put the cocoa in a sifter and shake it over the mixture, while you go on whipping, so you do not have any lumps. Continue until it is well blended. Whisk 3 egg whites until peaks form, then fold them in with a spatula. Whisk the cream until thickened, and gently fold in with the spatula.

Cut the ice cream into slices about 1.25cm (½ inch) thick and very quickly line the bottom and sides of an 800ml (1½ pint) basin. Pour in the mixture and freeze. You could cover the bottom with some more ice cream, in which case you will need another half block. When you want to use this dessert, just ease the sides with a pointed knife and turn it out on to a serving dish.

Decorate it with cream, glacé cherries or chocolate flakes, or anything else that you fancy.

Cannoli alla siciliana
Cannoli the Sicilian Way

Cannoli alla siciliana originated in Sicily, but they are made all over Italy. To make *cannoli* you need some moulds. You can buy them, made of tin, but it is easy to make some at home. Buy a length of wooden dowelling, 2cm (¾ inch) in diameter, cut it in sections about 14cm (5½ inches) long, sandpaper the ends and you have your moulds. Wash the moulds and let them dry before you use them.

Serves 6–8

For 12–13 cannoli
1 heaped teaspoon margarine
150g (6 oz) plain flour
salt
½ teaspoon sugar

125ml (4 fl oz) wine (white, red or fortified)
corn oil for frying
a little icing sugar

For the filling
220g (8 oz) ricotta
120g (5 oz) caster sugar
½ teaspoon vanilla essence

grated chocolate

Melt the margarine in a bowl over a saucepan of very hot water, then mix it with the flour, salt, sugar and make it into a stiff dough with the wine. Have some more flour handy, in case you need a little, to roll the dough into a ball. Cover and leave the dough to rest in a basin, covered with a cloth, for 1–1½ hours. Grease slightly the lengths of dowelling. After this time, roll out the dough in thin strips and cut squares of 10cm (4 inches) each side. Roll each piece around a piece of wood and close them by pressing with your fingers, one corner on top of the opposite one.

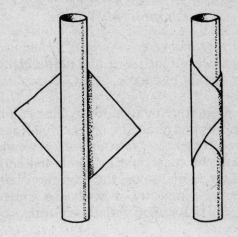

Heat the corn oil in a medium-sized frying pan. When sizzling, fry the *cannoli* on every side until golden brown. Cook 3 at a time, and turn them with the help of a pair of tongs. Do not cook them too quickly, as they must be dry and crisp.

You do not need to have the same number of moulds as the *cannoli* you are making, because a few minutes after you have cooked the first batch, you can gently remove them, cool under the cold tap, dry and use them again.

To make the filling, mix the ricotta with the caster sugar, and add the vanilla essence and a little grated plain or milk chocolate. When *cannoli* are cold, fill them with this mixture, either using a small spoon or a large piping nozzle. Dust the top with very little icing sugar. *Cannoli* must be eaten very soon after they are made or they will lose their crispness.

Cannoli (a modo mio)
Cannoli (My Way)

227g (8 oz) cream cheese   juice of ½ lemon
100g (4 oz) caster sugar   1 large Milk Flake,
½ teaspoon vanilla essence   crushed

This is an alternative method for making *cannoli*, using cream cheese instead of ricotta. Make *cannoli* as explained above. Soften the cheese, beating with a wooden spoon, together with the sugar, until smooth and creamy. Add vanilla and the lemon juice, then the chocolate. Pour in the cream cheese mixture, a little at a time, and mix thoroughly. Fill the *cannoli* with this mixture.

Castagnole

Castagnole are eaten at Carnival time. All regions of Italy have a dish typical of *Carnevale*, and *castagnole* is one common to many areas, although it may go under a different name in different places. There are lots of variations to the recipe for making *castagnole*. Housewives are always obsessed by the fact that they should rise a lot and be quite dry inside, so they keep adding their own contribution to the method which they think will help to achieve these results.

Serves 4–5

2 eggs
1 tablespoon caster sugar
1 tablespoon olive oil
grated rind of ½ lemon
2 tablespoons Mistrà
   (Italian aniseed liqueur)
   or whisky

self-raising flour to make a
   soft dough
cooking fat or oil for
   frying

Beat the eggs well in a large bowl with a hand whisk. Add the sugar and the oil and keep whisking for a few minutes, then add the lemon rind and liqueur. Mix in the flour, using a spatula, until a soft dough, which is smooth and thick but not hard, is formed. Heat the fat in a large frying pan. If the dough is a little sticky rub your hands in a little flour. Taking a small piece at a time, form into an oval shape and drop it into the boiling fat. Quickly make more *castagnole* and drop them in (not too many because they will swell a lot). As soon as there are enough in the pan, lower the heat and gently move the pan in a circular motion, lifting from the heat. Turn them once or twice and when they are a golden colour all over, lift them out and place on kitchen paper. Make sure you do not cook them too quickly. *Castagnole* should be very light and well cooked inside. Keep them hot while you cook the remaining batches. You will need to add some more cooking fat.

   Castagnole can be served just dusted with caster sugar or hot honey or with the following sauce.

Zabaglione sauce for castagnole

Whisk two egg yolks with 2 tablespoons caster sugar until they are fluffy and light. Very slowly, and while you are still beating, add one wineglass of Alchermes, sherry, Marsala or Madeira. Heat the sauce for a few minutes, placing the bowl over a pan of very hot water, while you stir it. When hot, pour it over the portions of hot *castagnole* with a spoon. Serve at once.

Cicerchiata

Serves 6–7

Same ingredients as for *castagnole* (page 253), plus

2 *tablespoons honey*	2 *tablespoons sugar, mixed*
1 *tablespoon cocoa*	*together*

This is a variation of *castagnole*. The name is derived from *cicerchia* which is a type of bean similar to chickpeas. It is so called because the pieces of pasta will be the size of a *cicerchia*.

Make the dough in the same way as for *castagnole*, but use a little more flour to make it more manageable. Take a small amount at a time and roll into a thin sausage shape, then cut into pieces the size of a halfpenny coin. Fry them and when they are golden in colour, take them out with a slotted spoon and drain on kitchen paper. Keep them hot until you finish frying them all. Now put the honey in a saucepan over moderate heat. Mix together well the cocoa and sugar. When the honey is boiling, add this mixture and stir well. Go on stirring all the time until the sugar is completely dissolved and the mixture is very runny. While it is boiling, tip the fried balls in the saucepan, stirring carefully with a wooden spoon until the balls are coated with the syrup. Remove from the heat. Turn your *cicerchiata* out on to a damp glass dish. Press the top down with a spatula so that they look like a cake. Leave to cool, then turn out on to a flat dish. Serve cold and cut in slices with a very sharp knife.

Frittelle
Fritters

Frittelle in Italy are made on 19 March, Saint Joseph's Day. This day is called *San Giuseppe frittellaio* – Saint Joseph, the fritter maker. In Naples they call them *zeppole*.

Serves 8–10

500ml (18 fl oz) water
250ml (8 fl oz) milk
75g (3 oz) butter
100g (4 oz) sugar
500g (20 oz) self-raising
  flour
6 eggs

grated rind of 1 lemon
1 teaspoon vanilla essence
2 tablespoons Mistrà
  (Italian aniseed liqueur)
oil for frying
4–5 tablespoons clear
  honey

Mix the water with the milk, heat it in a large saucepan over moderate heat with the butter and sugar. When it boils, drop in the flour, all in one go, mixing with a wooden spoon, until it becomes a dough in the shape of a ball. Remove the pan from the heat and let it cool down. When cold, add the eggs, one at a time, beating the mixture, then add the lemon rind, vanilla and Mistrà, until the mixture is smooth and velvety.

Heat the oil in a large frying pan; when sizzling, take pieces of the dough in your hands (about the size of one dessertspoon), mould them into a round shape using some extra flour and drop the fritters into the hot oil, turning them once, and fry them until golden. Make sure they are well cooked inside.

Lift them out with a fish slice and place them on kitchen paper. Keep them hot while you fry the remainder. Serve sprinkled with sugar or with melted honey. Heat the honey in a saucepan until it becomes very runny, then pour some over the fritters.

Turcata
Maize Flour Dessert

This pudding used to be cooked on an open fire in a revolving cake tin on three legs with a very long handle and a lid on which you put charcoal, for cooking the top. I still have one of those baking implements, which belonged to my great-grandmother.

I am not sure where it gets its name from, but it may well be because it is made from maize called *granturco* (wheat from Turkey). You can make *turcata* with some leftover polenta or you could cook some yellow flour first. When I want to make *turcata*, I make polenta the previous day, counting an extra portion, then when it is cooked, I save the extra amount in a basin until I am ready to make this. You need an 800ml (1½ pint) basin full of polenta (see page 169).

Dolci

Serves 8–10

1 large cooking apple
½ 120g (5 oz) packet dried
  figs
25g (1 oz) shelled walnuts
25g (1 oz) shelled almonds
50g (2 oz) sultanas
grated rind of ½ lemon

2 tablespoons olive oil
75g (3 oz) brown sugar
1 egg, lightly beaten
1 teaspoon ground
  cinnamon
½ teaspoon grated nutmeg

Tip the polenta into a mixing bowl and work it with a fork until it is smooth and creamy like custard. Peel the apple, cut it into small pieces, then chop the figs, walnuts and almonds and mix all together with the sultanas and the lemon rind. Mix the olive oil with the polenta and add the sugar, stirring well. Add the egg and spices.

Grease a 20cm (8 inch) cake tin and tip in the mixture. Bake in a preheated oven at 180°C (350°F), gas mark 4, for 1½ hours. Test it with a skewer which should come out just a little greasy, not sticky. When ready, leave it to cool a little before turning it out of the baking tin.

Ice Cream

'*E' arrivato il gelato veneziano*' you could hear the children shouting, and amid the general excitement and anticipated pleasure the deep voice of the vendor would go over the sound of the youngsters: '*Gelato veneziano!*' In my childhood, and for a long time afterwards, a great expectation for the day when this shout would be heard again would run amongst the younger generations every springtime. It was the beginning of the ice cream season when a family of three brothers, all from Venice, would journey south for some months every year to sell their ice creams. They took them around in their tricycles, which had 'Gelato Veneziano' written in bold letters across, and these carts had a container for the ice cream, surrounded by a space filled with crushed ice. People always think that the Neapolitans make the best ice creams, but this cannot be true, as I remember nothing better than the ice cream from Venice. There they sold small cornets, and larger cornets, but the most expensive ones consisted of a very thick slice of ice cream between two wafers. It was a real treat to get one of them, but the children's budget would very rarely stretch to spending the large sum of 10 *soldi* (50 cents = ½ lira) to buy one. There used to be three flavours, vanilla, chocolate and lemon. Nothing any fancier than that. A long cry from Howard Johnson's 58 flavours of transatlantic fame!

Ice cream making did not start in Italy, strange as it may sound, but in Paris, France. The person who invented it, though, was an Italian from southern Italy. He opened a restaurant and made the first ice creams there in the seventeenth century. They were very expensive to start with, but in a very short time they became so popular that their price was brought down to a realistic level and everybody could enjoy them. Now that ice-cream makers are available to the majority of housewives, it is relatively easy to make at home the flavours of your choice. The man was called Procopio, and the restaurant Procope, named after him, became famous in Paris, where it prospered until some years before the Second World War, when it was turned into a café.

Gelato alla crema or Fiordilatte
Dairy Ice Cream

This is the basis for many types of ice cream. You start with this plain dairy ice cream and add various flavours to make different ice creams.

3 *eggs*
3 *extra yolks*
100g (4 oz) *sugar*
1 *teaspoon vanilla essence*

1 *litre (1¾ pints) milk*
300ml (½ pint) *double*
   cream, lightly whipped

In a large mixing bowl, beat the eggs and sugar until fluffy, then add vanilla essence and mix well. Heat the milk to boiling point, then add it slowly to the eggs, mixing constantly. Return to the saucepan and stir until thickened, but *do not* boil. Leave this mixture to cool, fold in the cream then put it in an ice cream maker and follow the manufacturer's instructions. If you do not have an ice cream maker, set the freezing compartment of your refrigerator to its coldest setting. Place the mixture in a freezer tray and freeze until it starts to firm. Remove from the freezer, place in a large mixing bowl and whisk to break up the ice crystals. Repeat twice, then leave to freeze. To serve, transfer to the refrigerator for about 1 hour to soften slightly.

9

Torte e Biscotti
Cakes and Biscuits

Torta per compleanno
Birthday Cake

Birthday cakes, with candles to blow out and the singing of '*Buon compleanno a te*' (Happy Birthday to you) is a custom which was introduced in Italy after the Second World War, but although it was adopted very readily, the type of cake used at birthdays has resisted the foreign influence. No fruit cakes for birthdays – in fact Italians never make fruit cakes the way they are made in the UK. I find it very amusing when Italian friends are present at a celebration where a fruit cake is cut. They look at the small pieces served and I know in their mind they're thinking how mean people are. Only later do they realize how filling a piece of good fruit cake can be and they are glad not to have got the big piece they expected at first! A birthday cake is usually a sort of sponge cake filled with cream or a chocolate cake or a *millefoglie* (a thousand leaves).

Millefoglie
Thousand Leaves Cake

Millefoglie is made with flaky pastry and a filling which can be of cream or fruit. If you do not want to make the flaky pastry, buy a good brand.

If you need to blanch the almonds, put them in a saucepan and bring them to the boil. Remove from the heat and take out one by one taking the skin off. Rinse them and dry. Spread them on an oven tray and put them in a moderate heat until very dry and hardly coloured. Leave them to cool then chop up in small chips.

Serves 8–10

For the pastry
350g (12 oz) plain flour *300ml (½ pint) water*
a pinch of salt
350g (12 oz) butter, well
    chilled

For the filling
3 egg yolks *100ml (3½ fl oz) double*
90g (3½ oz) sugar *cream*
75g (3 oz) plain flour *100g (4 oz) blanched*
500ml (18 fl oz) milk *almonds or almond*
1 tablespoon Marsala or any *chips*
    liqueur you like *icing sugar*
a small stick of cinnamon *glacé cherries*
a small strip of lemon rind

Sift the flour and salt into a large mixing bowl. Divide the butter into 4 portions. Return three quarters of the butter to the refrigerator. Put one quarter into the flour and rub in with your fingertips until the mixture resembles fine breadcrumbs. Add the water and mix with a palette knife until a soft dough is formed, then turn it out on to a floured board. Knead it until all the cracks are gone. Roll the dough into an oblong shape and wrap in cling film, then refrigerate for 15 minutes. Dice the second portion of butter lightly and place in the middle of the oblong. Fold the top third of the oblong down, then fold the bottom third up. Roll with a rolling pin in one direction until the butter is well incorporated. Cover and set aside for 20 minutes. Make another oblong shape and proceed in the same way with the remaining pieces of butter. When you have used up all the butter, roll out a couple of times more, folding the pastry in three every time. Leave the pastry to cool, while you prepare the filling for the *millefoglie*.

Beat the egg yolks with the sugar. Mix the flour with a little of the milk, then mix with the eggs. Give it a good whisk, then pour into a large saucepan and add the remaining milk with the Marsala, cinnamon and lemon rind. Heat slowly, stirring all the time as it thickens, until it reaches boiling point. Boil for a few moments, then remove from the heat, removing the lemon rind and cinnamon. Pour into a basin to cool. Stir from time to time so a skin does not form on the top.

Divide the pastry into four pieces. Grease a baking sheet. Roll out the first piece about 3mm (⅛ inch) thick into a circular shape about 20cm (8 inches) in diameter. Use a pointed knife to make a more regular circle. Slide the circle carefully on to the baking sheet, prick the surface all over with the prongs of a fork, then bake it in an oven at 230°C (450°F), gas mark 8, until it starts turning golden (about 20 minutes). Cool down on a wire rack. Cool the oven tin before you cook the next circle of pastry. Bake the four circles, then, using all the cuttings from the first four, roll out this pastry again and make the fifth circle. When you have baked the five circles of pastry, place one on a large round dish, making sure the size and shape is the same as the others. You can trim with a very sharp pointed knife if necessary. Spread on this circle a quarter of the cream, place another circle on top, and so on, until you use all the pastry. Leave a very small amount of the cream to spread very thinly around the sides of the cake, so that, with the palm of your hand, you can take some almond chips to stick to it.

Sift a little icing sugar over the top of the cake. Whip the remaining cream till very fluffy and decorate the cake with it, spreading it with the blade of a knife. Decorate with some glacé cherries in a circle.

Torta di cioccolato con biscotti [F]
Chocolate Cake with Biscuits

2 eggs, separated
175g (6 oz) unsalted butter
175g (6 oz) drinking chocolate
100g (4 oz) roasted hazelnuts, crushed

225g (8 oz) biscuits, Rich Tea type, finely crushed
1 extra egg white
whipped cream and chocolate flakes, to serve

Add the egg yolks one by one to the butter, beating all the time. Add the drinking chocolate and mix well to avoid getting any lumps. Add the nuts and biscuits to the mixture. Beat the egg whites until stiff, then fold them in with a spatula.

Line any dish you want your cake to take the shape of with greaseproof paper and turn the mixture into it. Cover the top with another sheet of paper and press down with a lid or a plate that fits exactly into the dish. Put a small weight on top and leave it overnight in the refrigerator. Next day turn it on to a serving dish and cover it with whipped cream. Decorate with chocolate flakes.

Torta al Marsala [Ⓕ]
Marsala Cake

You can divide it into two smaller cakes, use one and freeze one. Amaretto is a favourite Italian almond-flavoured liqueur. The best is *Amaretto di Saronno*.

Serves 10–12

4 tablespoons caster sugar
100g (4 oz) unsalted
   butter
4 egg yolks
2 tablespoons Amaretto
24 trifle sponge cakes

1 glass Marsala mixed with
   1 tablespoon Amaretto
150ml (¼ pint) whipped
   cream
glacé cherries

For the custard
1 egg
1 tablespoon sugar

1 tablespoon flour
300ml (½ pint) milk

Start by making some custard. Beat 1 egg and 1 tablespoon of sugar together. Mix the flour with a little of the milk, then mix the remaining milk with the egg mixture. Place in a saucepan over a moderate heat, stirring all the time, until it boils and thickens. Boil it for a few moments, then remove from the heat and set aside to cool, stirring often so it does not form a skin on top.

Beat the caster sugar with the butter until very creamy and fluffy. Add one yolk of egg at a time and go on whisking, then add 2 tablespoons Amaretto. When the custard is really cold, mix it into this mixture. Grease a 25×6cm (10×2½ inch) ovenproof dish and line with greaseproof paper. Cut the sponge cakes in half horizontally to line the bottom of the dish and sprinkle with some of the Marsala and Amaretto. Evenly spread some of the cake mixture over the sponges. Make a second layer of sponges and sprinkle with Marsala and Amaretto, then the mixture and so on until you have finished all the ingredients. It is best to end up with a cake layer, but this is not really essential. (If you end up with the mixture on the top layer, just put the cake in the fridge for a little while to make this layer set, before covering it with a sheet of greaseproof paper.) Cover with a sheet of greaseproof paper, then a lid or a flat plate that fits exactly on top of the paper. Put a weight on top, and refrigerate overnight. Turn the cake out on to a serving dish and decorate with whipped cream and glacé cherries.

To freeze this cake, cover with the greaseproof paper, and the lid and weight, but do not refrigerate. Leave overnight at room temperature. Remove the lid, wrap the cake and its container in foil, seal, label and freeze. To serve, defrost for 6–7 hours at room temperature, then decorate.

Pan di spagna ⓕ
Sponge Cake

Serves 8–10

5 *eggs, separated*
175g (6 oz) sugar

150g (5 oz) self-raising
flour, sifted

Beat the egg yolks and the sugar until light and fluffy. Add the flour gradually. Beat the egg whites until stiff, then fold them into the cake mixture. Grease a 25cm (10 inch) cake tin. Tip the mixture in and bake in a preheated oven at 190°C (375°F), gas mark 5, for about 45 minutes. After 25 minutes, check that the top is not getting too brown. If it is, cover with a piece of foil. Test with a long needle to see if it's ready: the needle should come out dry. Cool for 10 minutes in the tin, then turn out on to a wire rack to cool completely.

Torta diplomatica
Diplomatic Cake

Usually there are small cakes called *diplomatici*. Maybe their name derives from the fact that they are a sort of compromise, a mixture of something taken from one sweet and some from another – a diplomatic assortment!

Make the flaky pastry as in the recipe for *Millefoglie* (page 262), and a sponge cake as in *Pan di spagna* above. Cool.

You can make a large square cake and cut it into 5cm (2 inch) squares, just as they are sold in pastry shops in Italy. To make a cake for ten portions you need two large circles of flaky pastry, and a sponge cake.

Serves 10

For the cream
3 egg yolks
3 tablespoons sugar
2 tablespoons plain flour
500ml (18 fl oz) milk
a strip of lemon rind

a small stick of cinnamon
1 tumbler Alchermes
icing sugar and candied
fruit for decoration

Beat the eggs with the sugar until light and fluffy. In a separate basin, mix the flour with 2 tablespoons of the milk, then add this to the egg mixture. Mix well and place everything in a saucepan over moderate heat with the rest of the milk, lemon rind and cinnamon. Stir continuously while the cream warms and thickens. Boil just for a second or two. Remove from the heat and leave to cool, stirring from time to time.

When the sponge is cold, slice it into two circles horizontally. Place one circle of the pastry on a large flat dish. Spread one third of the cream on it. Place the first half of the sponge cake on this. Sprinkle the sponge with some of the Alchermes. Spread another third of the cream and on top place the other half of the sponge cake, sprinkling it with Alchermes. Spread the rest of the cream, and place the other circle of pastry on top. Sieve some icing sugar and add some candied fruit as decoration.

Torta di nozze
Wedding Cake

An Italian wedding cake is often a St Honorè, which is a flaky pastry cake, with cream surrounded by *bignè* (profiteroles), covered in caramel.

Serves 8–10

For the pastry
175g (6 oz) butter   *175g (6 oz) plain flour*
150ml (¼ pint) water

For the filling
4 *eggs*
175g (6 oz) sugar
100g (4 oz) flour
1 litre (1¾ pints) milk

2 teaspoons brandy
(optional)
2 tablespoons cocoa

For the *bignè*
150ml (¼ pint) water
50g (2 oz) butter
pinch of salt

75g (3 oz) self-raising
flour
2 eggs

For the caramel sauce
100g (4 oz) sugar
2 tablespoons water

50g (2 oz) melted chocolate
(optional)

Make the flaky pastry (see page 263). You will need a circle of about 30cm (12 inches) in diameter, and 1cm (⅓ inch) thick. Grease a baking sheet and place the circle on it, with the help of a rolling pin or you may tear it. Bake it for 15 minutes in a preheated oven at 220°C (425°F), gas mark 7. Leave it to cool on a wire rack.

Make the *bignè* as described on page 277. Cream together the eggs, sugar, flour and milk. Add a little brandy if desired and mix well. Leave to cool. If you mix some cocoa into half of the cream you will have a mixture of *bignè*. (Mix only a little of the cream at a time with the cocoa to avoid any lumps.) Fill all the *bignè* when cold. Pour the rest of the cream (there will be quite a lot) on top of the flaky pastry dish and spread it evenly.

Make a hot caramel sauce by melting the sugar and the chocolate if using, in the water. When you have filled the *bignè*, dip one at a time into the hot caramel, then place them in a circle around the cake on top of the cream. Put a cherry on top of every *bignè*, and fill the middle with some whipped cream.

Ciambellone [F]
Ring-Shaped Cake

Ciambellone takes its name from *ciambella*, a ring. It is, in fact, a cake in the shape of a big ring. It is baked in a cake tin with a 'funnel' in the middle, or in an ordinary tin with an upturned greased object placed in the middle. This has always been my children's favourite at teatime, just as they got home from school, and now my grandchildren love it too.

150g (6 oz) butter
2 eggs
275g (10 oz) sugar
grated rind of 1 lemon
250ml (8 fl oz) milk

about 275g (10 oz) self-
  raising flour
1 teaspoon vanilla essence
1 teaspoon baking powder

Melt the butter by standing it in a basin placed in a saucepan of boiling water. In a large mixing bowl, beat the eggs well, then add the sugar and the melted butter. Mix well, adding the lemon rind, the milk and continue mixing with a wooden spoon. Start adding a few spoonfuls of flour and add enough to make a very soft dough. Lastly, add the vanilla essence and the baking powder, mixing well.

Pour the mixture into a greased 20cm (8 inch) cake tin. Bake in a preheated oven at 200°C (400°F), gas mark 6, for 30–45 minutes. The cake is cooked if a skewer inserted in the centre comes out clean. Place the cake on a wire rack and leave to cool. It is good even while still warm.

Crostata Ⓕ
Lattice Jam Tart

For the pastry

*350g (12 oz) self-raising
    flour*
175g (6 oz) sugar
*175g (6 oz) butter or
    margarine*

grated rind of 1 lemon
*2 eggs and 1 egg yolk,
    lightly beaten*

For the top

*350g (12 oz) jam of your
    choice*

1 egg white, to glaze

Rub flour, sugar and fat together, adding the lemon rind and mixing with the beaten eggs. Make a ball out of this dough, wrap in a cloth, and leave in a cool place for 30 minutes. Grease a 25cm (10 inch) flan dish. Roll out the pastry on a lightly floured surface and use about two-thirds to line the bottom and sides of the dish. Spread over the jam, covering the bottom with a thick layer – not too thick or it will boil over, but you should not be able to see the pastry at all. Use the remaining pastry to make a decorative lattice work on top and finish off the edges, all the way round, with a small roll of pastry so that the jam does not spill over when cooking. Brush the pastry with the beaten remaining egg white. Bake it in a preheated oven at 190°C (375°F), gas mark 5, for about 30–45 minutes. Make sure that the bottom pastry is as cooked as the top. It is best to use a glass dish, so that you can look at the bottom. Leave it to cool before cutting into slices to serve.

Tortiglione
Twisted Cake

Serves 6–8

For the pastry

100ml (3½ fl oz) water
50g (2 oz) butter
275g (10 oz) self-raising
  flour

1 egg, lightly beaten
a pinch of salt

For the filling

2 large cooking apples,
  peeled, cored and sliced
juice of 1 lemon
4 tablespoons sugar
1 tablespoon cocoa
2 tablespoons olive oil
2 tablespoons jam
120g (5 oz) dried figs
50g (2 oz) sultanas

25g (1 oz) currants
25g (1 oz) walnuts,
  chopped
25g (1 oz) hazelnuts or
  almonds, chopped
50g (2 oz) fresh white
  breadcrumbs
milk
brown sugar

Sprinkle the apple slices with a little lemon juice and half of the sugar. To make the pastry, heat the water and melt the butter in it. Put the flour into a basin, making a well in the centre. When the water is warm and the butter is melted, tip it into the well. Mix quickly with a fork, then add the egg and salt and make the dough into a ball. Heat a basin by immersing it in boiling water, dry it and place, upturned, over the dough, and leave to rest for 30 minutes.

In a basin mix the cocoa with the remaining sugar. Work a little of the pastry with your hands, using flour to prevent it sticking. Roll out the pastry on a cloth on a table, making it as thin as you can, without tearing it. Brush the olive oil all over the pastry, sprinkle the cocoa-sugar mixture evenly and dot the jam all over. Do not try to spread the jam or you will tear the pastry. Spread the fruit and nuts on top, leaving about 2.5cm (1 inch) border all round. Lastly, sprinkle over the breadcrumbs. Now very carefully lift one corner of the cloth under the pastry and with both hands, roll it to make a sausage shape, sticking the edge together with the other side of the pastry. Brush with a little milk to help the edges stick. Twist the sausage around while you press with your hands, so there is no air trapped in it. This 'twist' should give it the shape that the name *tortiglione* suggests.

Place it on a large, flat baking sheet and arrange into a horseshoe shape. Brush the top with milk and sprinkle with some brown sugar. Bake it in a preheated oven at 180°C (350°F), gas mark 4, for 45 minutes. Leave it to cool a little before cutting into slices. It is just as good warm or cold.

Crostata alla crema
Fruit and Cream Tart
Serves 6–8

For the custard
2 *eggs*
2 *tablespoons sugar*
2 *tablespoons cornflour*
500ml (18 fl oz) *milk*

a small strip lemon rind
a small stick cinnamon

For the *crostata*
225g (8 oz) *self-raising flour*
100g (4 oz) *butter or margarine*
100g (4 oz) *sugar*
1 *egg, lightly beaten*

1 *egg yolk*
peaches, apricots or fresh fruit of your choice
50ml (2 fl oz) *double cream*

Make the custard first. Beat the eggs with the sugar. Dissolve the cornflour in 2 tablespoons of milk, then mix together with the beaten eggs and the rest of the milk. Stir well, add the lemon rind and the cinnamon and pour into a large saucepan over moderate heat. Heat, stirring constantly until the mixture comes to the boil and thickens. Remove from the heat and leave it to cool, stirring from time to time. Discard the cinnamon and lemon rind.

Make the pastry by rubbing flour, butter and sugar together with your fingertips until the mixture resembles fine breadcrumbs. Add the egg and mix into a rough dough. On a lightly floured surface, roll out the pastry to line a greased 20cm (8 inch) flan dish. Prick the base of the pastry and cook for 20 minutes in a preheated oven at 190°C (375°F), gas mark 5. Allow the pastry to cool completely, then pour in the cold custard. Peel, stone and quarter the peaches or apricots (or prepare any other fruit of your choice) and decoratively arrange on top of the custard. Finish off by decorating with some whipped cream.

Pizza 'margherita'
'Daisy' Cake

In this case the term *pizza* means cake. This is a fat-free sponge cake.

5 eggs, separated
175g (6 oz) caster sugar
175g (6 oz) potato flour

1 teaspoon vanilla essence
grated rind of ½ lemon
1 teaspoon baking powder

Beat the egg yolks with sugar until thick. Add the flour, the vanilla essence, the lemon rind and baking powder. Beat the whites still stiff, then fold them into the batter. Grease and flour a 25cm (10 inch) cake tin, about 5cm (2 inches) deep. Pour in the mixture and bake for about 15 minutes in a preheated oven at 240°C (425°F), gas mark 9. Reduce the heat to 160°C (325°F), gas mark 3, and bake for a further 20–25 minutes. When the cake is cooked, a skewer inserted in the centre will come out clean.

Biscotti della Befana
Befana Biscuits

Makes about 60

225g (8 oz) butter
100g (4 oz) sugar
350g (12 oz) self-raising flour

grated rind of ½ lemon
1 teaspoon vanilla essence
1 egg, lightly beaten

Melt the butter in a basin over hot water, then mix with the sugar, flour, lemon, vanilla essence and lastly the egg. Roll the dough into a ball. Lightly grease a baking sheet, or two if you want to cook more biscuits at the same time, as they will not all fit on to one sheet. On a lightly floured surface, roll out the pastry to the thickness of about 3mm (⅛ inch). With some fancy biscuit cutters, cut out the shapes until you use up all the pastry. Gather up the leftover strips, roll them out again together, and cut some more shapes. Bake these biscuits in a preheated oven at 160°C (325°F), gas mark 3, for 20 minutes. They should be a lovely golden colour.

Bignè Ⓕ
Profiteroles

These *bignè* can be used for savoury dishes (see page 56) as well as for sweet ones. You fill them, when cold, by making an incision on the side with a very sharp knife and inserting the filling with a piping nozzle. As sweets you can fill them with custard, or with cream, or with a chocolate mixture. You can add a little liqueur to the filling for extra zest.

Makes 24

150ml (5 fl oz) water
a pinch of salt
50g (2 oz) butter

75g (3 oz) self-raising
  flour
2 eggs

Heat the water, salt and butter together in a saucepan. When the butter is melted and the water boils, remove it from the heat and pour in all the flour at once, mixing with a wooden spoon. Return to the heat for a few moments, stirring all the time, then set aside to cool. Add the eggs one at a time, beating well after each addition. Go on beating until the pastry is very smooth and velvety.

Grease a baking sheet and put small amounts of pastry on it with a dessert spoon. Leave plenty of room in between as they expand during baking. Bake them in a preheated oven at 220°C (425°F), gas mark 7, for 15 minutes. They should be a golden colour and firm to the touch, but if they are not, leave them for 3–4 minutes longer. Turn the oven off and leave them in for 10 minutes, say, or they might deflate. Leave them to completely cool on a wire rack.

Biscotti con mosto [Ⓕ]
Biscuits with Must

Mosto is the new wine, when it is still cloudy, soon after the grapes have been pressed. These biscuits are made around September–October when the must is available.

Makes 30–35

50g (2 oz) fresh yeast	*500g (1 lb) sugar*
50ml (2 fl oz) water	*100g (4 oz) aniseed*
350g (12 oz) plain flour	*2 litres (3½ pints) must*
500ml (18 fl oz) olive oil	*1 egg white*

Put the fresh yeast in a basin with the water and 3 tablespoons flour. Mix well and leave it overnight. The next morning, mix with the remaining flour, oil, sugar, aniseed and the must. Leave the dough to rise.

Cut the pieces of dough and roll them in the shape of long sausages, 3cm (1¼ inches) thick. Take the middle of the sausage shape and twist the two ends together. Place on a greased baking sheet. Brush the tops with egg white. Bake in a preheated oven at 200°C (400°F), gas mark 6, for 30–40 minutes.

Fave dei morti
Broad Beans of the Dead

The name given to these biscuits, which are a type of macaroon, comes from All Saints' and All Souls' Day, the first and second days of November when they are made.

These two days are also called *I Morti* – The Dead – because they are dedicated to the deceased. A crowd is constantly visiting the cemeteries. Everybody goes at one time or another. There are meetings for prayers, and the chapel is open for a yearly service. The days prior to the first of November are very busy, too, and the cemeteries are crowded with people cleaning and polishing, and bringing flowers. Chrysanthemums are the November flower which will adorn the cemeteries, usually the very large ball-like variety which are grown especially to be marketed just before this date. Italians will not have chrysanthemums in their houses, because of the connotation. The first time I was given an enormous bouquet of chrysanthemums, after I had my first baby, I threw them out thinking, 'They want me dead here!'

I think these biscuits are probably made at this time because the almonds have just been harvested and are at their best.

Makes 35–40

a knob of butter (the size of a walnut)
100g (4 oz) almonds
150g (6 oz) sugar
75g (3 oz) self-raising flour

2 teaspoons ground cinnamon
grated rind of ½ lemon
1 egg, beaten

Melt the butter in a basin standing in boiling water. Mix the almonds with the sugar, then add the flour, cinnamon, lemon rind, and melted butter and the egg. Mix slowly until you get a smooth dough. Grease a baking sheet, sprinkle it with flour, then shake off the surplus. Roll the pastry into a long sausage, about 2.5cm (1 inch) thick. Cut it into sections, then squash each piece to 1cm (½ inch) thick, giving it an oval shape, the shape of a broad bean.

Cook in a preheated oven at 160°C (325°F), gas mark 3, for about 20 minutes. They should be golden in colour.

Caffè
Coffee

And when you have finished an Italian dinner, treat yourself and your guests to a good cup of coffee, Italian roasted and freshly ground. As an old Italian saying goes, 'Coffee should be dark as the night, strong as a man, sweet as a young lady.' A very good addition to it is a dash of Mistrà, which acts as a digestive and will take care of any over-indulgence on your part!

Italian Food Shops

Cambridge Delicatessen 9 Broadway Mill Road,
    Cambridge
Camisa & Son 61 Old Compton Street, London W1
Continental Specialities St Martin's Arcade, Birmingham
Elite Delicatessen 60 The Broadway, Tolworth, Surrey
Fazzi Brothers Ltd 230–232 Clyde Street, Glasgow
Frosts Food Stores 1 Wimbledon Hill Road, Wimbledon,
    SW19
Frosts Food Stores 141 Putney High Street, Putney, SW15
Gate Delicatessen 343 Archway Road, London N6
Gazzano & Son 169 Farringdon Road, London EC1
Licata & Son 36 Picton Street, Montepellier, Bristol
Lina Stores 18 Brewer Street, London W1
Luigi's Delicatessen 349 Fulham Road, London SW10
Olga Stores 412 Harrow Road, London W9
O'Sullivan Ltd 11 Duke Street, Dublin
Parmigiani & Figli 36a Old Brompton Street, London W1
Pasta Bar 313 Fulham Road, London SW3
Terroni Luigi & Sons 138 Clerkenwell Road, London EC1
Valvona e Crolla 19 Elm Row, Edinburgh 7
Waitrose Supermarkets

Pasta-making machines and espresso machines can be
purchased from Lega Ltd, 107 Fortis Green, London N2. The
price of an ordinary pasta machine, at the time of writing,
is £12.85.

Index

Ⓕ denotes recipes which may be frozen

Index

Index

Index

Index

Index